PENNINE BRANCH LINES

PENNINE BRANCH LINES

ALAN EARNSHAW

IAN ALLAN
Publishing

Contents

First published 1993

ISBN 0 7110 2171 6

Published by Ian Allan Ltd, Shepperton, Surrey; and printed by Ian Allan Printing Ltd at its works at Coombelands in Runnymede, England.

Introduction

As every horticulturist knows, a tree needs both roots and branches to survive. These help it gather the nutrients it needs to thrive, they furnish it with strong foundations to withstand any onslaught, they bestow shelter and in general both promote and generate further growth. This basic philosophy is also true of railways, for without strong roots and branches the main trunk would wither and slowly die. As our railway system slithers, stumbles and falls into privatisation, it is quite clear that the trunk is dying. Indeed one does not even have to be an astute follower of railway history to realise that our national system is very sick; in fact if it were a tree, it would have a better chance of recovering from Dutch Elm Disease. The malaise that has stifled railway development from Beeching onwards is often laid at the door of the road transport industry, and whilst this is true, in many ways the blame for the railway's failure must fairly be rested upon the shoulders of successive Ministers of Transport and senior railway management alike.

At the time of writing we have a Government White Paper that sees no rôle for freight operations within BR, whilst there is a keen desire to hive off to the private sector whatever profitable services that can be disposed of. As a sop to the travelling public, noises are being made about the support of services considered to be socially necessary. Whilst this promised 'support' may be perceived as being the current thinking, did we not hear precisely the self same promises on the de-regulation (fiasco) of bus services a few years ago. As one leading back-bench MP on the Government side of the House recently commented to me, 'Privatisation is an experiment with one of our most important national assets, it will do nothing but lead to the fragmentation and eventual demise of a socially oriented railway system'. True, similar words were spoken after Beeching wielded his mighty axe, and some might counter that the railways are still here. Still here they may be, but we may be justified asking, in what shape? As Beeching chopped away at the branches, he irreparably damaged the body of the tree. Whilst the national network appeared to survive reasonably intact, terminal rot had set in.

In the heartlands of the South Pennines, the railways figured large in both the social and industrial development of the area, bringing with them prosperity, expansion and social reform. The advent of a branch line to a small community like Meltham or Bacup did more than provide a means of getting people into the neighbouring towns more quickly, it gave the impetus for industrialisation by establishing the all-important arteries on which freight traffic might develop. Prior to the coming of the turnpikes and the canals, much of the area's traditional industry, textiles, had been confined to small manufacturing communities, many of which were located in hilltop settlements. Abundant supplies of soft, clean water were an essential part of the textile manufacturing process, not least for washing the wool crop or powering waterwheels. However, with better communications, coal was soon being transported along valley bottom routes and riverside mills sprang up to take advantage of a new power source - steam. Great engines were built to power the mills, with miles of endless belts driving the individual pieces of machinery. Despite the nefarious activities of the Luddites, the industrial revolution had taken place.

The railways were to take advantage of this development, and within a few years the main lines that passed through the area were radiating branches into previously untapped districts. The growth was both phenomenal and incalculable; mills, mines, quarries, steel works, iron foundries and brick-works all springing up to fuel the growing development. In this book we will consider around a score of branch lines in the South Pennines, thereby presenting an overall picture of how the local railway network developed. It can not be a full account, in just 128 pages we are hard pressed to present an outline of the branches under consideration. Yet it is intended that this work will serve as a tribute to recall how important these lines once were, not only to the communities they served but to the national rail network as well. A few of the lines are still served by BR trains, though for how long these will remain is anyone's guess. Three of the branch lines now house private railways and all credit to the groups and individuals behind these efforts, for their actions present the story far better than any written words or frozen images on a printed page. Elsewhere the legacy of our rich heritage is disappearing under a cloak of weeds and shrubbery, or perhaps being buried under the concrete floor of a new supermarket or industrial development. Accordingly, in our selection of pictures we have tried to bring the story up to date, by showing what has happened on these lines since their closure; in some instances it will be difficult for the reader to appreciate that there was a railway line there at all.

Nevertheless this book has been an enjoyable trip down memory lane, taking me back on lines where I made furtive trips in the back of a guard's van, on a footplate or where I just crept along wall sides to avoid being spotted by some vigilant railwayman. With the exception of the Barnoldswick and Rochdale-Bacup branches, I travelled along all or part of these branches in my youth. So in some ways, besides its historical brief, this book is a bit of a nostalgia trip. I hope you enjoy it now as much as I did then.

Alan Earnshaw,
Shepley,
Huddersfield,
March 1993.

Acknowledgements

In any book project the author, who usually gets most of the praise, must rely on a substantial level of support from an unseen network of contributors. This is certainly true of this book, for without the willing help and assistance of a number of people and organisations, this work would not have been possible. It never ceases to amaze me how many people willingly come forward to help, particularly those who do so with no expectation of great financial reward and thereby do it for the love of the subject. Railway publishing has always been a marginal business, and I am deeply indebted to those who have expended their time, money and energy on helping me with the production of this account. I have made several new friends in the course of the work, and to these ones I am particularly grateful that they have entrusted their precious photographs into the hands of a complete stranger. To name all who have assisted would be impossible, but I must record those who have been of the greatest assistance. So my thanks go to: John Alcock, Phillip Atkins, Oliver Carter, Gordon Coultas, Jim Davenport, Bob Essery, Bury Metropolitan Council, *Bury Times*, Richard S. Greenwood, *Huddersfield Daily Examiner*, Robin Higgins, David Ibbotson, Barry C. Lane, Gavin Morrison, *Oldham Chronicle*, Bill Rear, Paul Shannon, Peter Sunderland, Brian Taylor and Graham Veevers. Also the staff of the National Railway Museum, Public Records Office, Kew, the reference/local studies libraries of Barnsley, Bradford, Bury, Colne, Glossop, Halifax, Huddersfield, Keighley, Oldham, Penistone, Rochdale, Skipton and the West Yorkshire and Lancashire archive services. I am also mindful of the assistance given by Myles Handy of Wear Valley Council, who gave up his own time during a visit to Shepperton to help me go through the Ian Allan library files in search of suitable illustrations. Finally it is fitting to pay tribute to my daughter Sarah who assisted with my research, and to the rest of my family who have helped so much. In conclusion may I say a sincere thank you to my wife/secretary Larraine, to whom I dedicate this book with all my love and thanks for her continued support.

1 The Glossop Branch

Conception & Construction

The development of the Glossop service is, in many ways, unique — not least because of the fact that it is still one of the few true branch lines still operated into the Pennines by British Rail. It is prudent to begin our journey round the branches along this line, even though some readers might feel that this is a branch in the Peak District. However, a look at any Ordnance Survey map will reveal that Glossop is outside the National Park area and, thereby, more rightly associated with the South Pennines as a whole rather than the Peak District in particular. Anyway it is one of my favourite branches, so here it is.

Train services for Glossop were first provided by the Sheffield, Ashton-under-Lyne & Manchester Railway, who were to open their route from Manchester to Sheffield in successive stages. On 24 December 1842 the line had reached the west end of Dinting Vale, where a temporary station bearing the name Glossop was opened. Of course, it was quite some distance away from the town itself and, in those days, such matters were taken with a great deal of licence anyway. The work on the

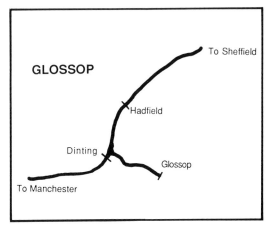

1,452ft-long Dinting Vale Viaduct precluded any immediate extension eastward. This remained the case until 7 August 1844 when the terminus was extended up to Woodhead. Through running to Sheffield came even later, with the Woodhead Tunnel not being ready for opening until 22 December 1845.

Right:
Class K3 2-6-0 on a duplicate Marylebone-Manchester with 'N5' 0-6-2T at the rear. The 'N5s' were regular performers on the Glossop branch prior to electrification, but even the most ardent admirers would admit that they were a bit long in the tooth by this time. Jim Farrell recalls a time when a Cleethorpes train of 12 coaches failed at Dinting one October evening in 1949, and No 69308 was used to take the train over Woodhead to Sheffield, quite an arduous task for a diminutive tank engine. *The late Frank Alcock*

Left:
The junction station is well illustrated in this view as Class B1 4-6-0 No 61167 passes through Dinting with a Fallowfield-Barnsley (Courthouse) football special on 7 April 1950. *The late Frank Alcock*

Below left:
Former GCR Class C13, the work-horses of the branch in pre-electrification days, leaves Dinting on a Glossop-Manchester local on 7 April 1950. Recently repainted in British Railways livery with straight lettering and no crest, the old LNER emblem can just be seen beneath the new coat of paint. *The late Frank Alcock*

Below:
A train formed of Great Central tank and rake of six-wheel coaches heads across Dinting Viaduct before the bridge was strengthened. This photograph is an interesting contrast with the later shot of No 43929 crossing the same viaduct after the completion of the 1,500V dc electrification scheme. *Bucknall Collection/Ian Allan Library*

The Glossop branch itself is something of an enigma, for its construction and opening were accomplished without any Act of Parliament. The line was built by, and on land entirely belonging to, the Duke of Norfolk — a fact which the stone lion outside the station at Glossop still brings to our attention. At this time the town had already become established as a prominent manufacturing centre, with mills and factories springing up all along the banks of the streams and rivers issuing forth from the boggy plateau of Kinder Scout which stands sentinel above the town.

From the outset the line was worked by the SA&MR, but one significant factor was the renaming of the station on the main line from Glossop to Dinting. Even so this was a shortlived station, it closed in 1847 when it was replaced by a station at the junction of the branch. Goods trains began on 9 June 1845, but difficulties over the junction's layout prevented the commencement of passenger trains for three weeks. In 1846 the branch was sold by the Duke of Norfolk to the SA&MR. The single-line branch proved to be something of a bottleneck, mainly due to the fact that the junction originally faced in an easterly direction. For several years the locals agitated for improvements, including a junction facing Manchester. These were eventually provided in 1884 when the line was doubled, and the west-facing spur installed. Of course, this meant that Dinting station was once again in the wrong place, so it was moved into the 'V' formed by the main line and the Manchester arm of the junction.

The Line Described

Having crossed Dinting Vale Viaduct, the Woodhead line heads in a northeasterly direction, coming almost immediately to the west-facing arm of the Glossop branch junction. To the left stood the engine shed, better known to many railway enthusiasts in its later life as the Dinting Railway Centre. The story of how it became the home to the group determined to preserve ex-LMS 'Jubilee' class 4-6-0 *Bahamas* is well known, as is its demise and the eventual movement of much of the stock to the Keighley & Worth Valley Railway. It is sad that this superbly valiant effort at railway preservation foundered, but it remains a salutary lesson of what can happen to even the most promising of schemes. As I watched the last of those engines move from Dinting, my heart went out to all those who had laboured so long and so hard, but yet in vain. I also recalled the grand vision they had of running steam up the Woodhead line on a regular basis, after BR had decided they had no further need of the route.

Moving quickly away from the site of the old engine shed/railway centre complex, the Manchester arm of the line joins with the eastern arm of the original branch. It then runs on for some little distance to where it is crossed by the road leading from Higher Dinting. Heading now in a east-south-east direction, the line ambles past Lower Dinting and on to the terminus at Glossop. No intermediate stations were served and, today, only a single platform exists for the EMUs that operate the services to Hadfield and Manchester. The rest of the site has been taken over by a Co-operative store and the goods yard converted to a car park. The lion still stands outside the station, but its roar seems to be less now than in childhood days when I travelled from Huddersfield via Penistone to visit my great uncle and aunt. For many years he had been a locomotive superintendent at Gorton but he retired in August 1939. With the outbreak of war the following month he was appointed as a Railway Transport Officer and given control over the Woodhead route. Accordingly, his last years in the railway service were spent supervising the movement of munition traffic through Woodhead Tunnel during World War 2. His recollections were always of interest as he regaled us with stories of how they used to put important trains into the tunnel during the air raids to keep them from harm. One night they had Prime Minister Winston Churchill's train secure in the tunnel, without anyone realising that two trains of high explosive shells were stabled in the adjoining bore. The memories of the visits conjure up images of darkened drawing rooms, the smell of mothballs and idle chatter about the exploits of railway managers long since deceased — I wouldn't have changed it for the world. If my interest in railways began anywhere, it was in Talbot Street, Glossop.

Services and Demise

Throughout its life, and up to the demise of the main line to Sheffield, the branch was always an extremely useful little appendage grafted on to the side of the Woodhead route. Little is known about the early working of the branch other than its operation being 'one engine in steam' until 1884/85, similarly details of motive power and coaching stock are also scarce. However, it is known that the line was the home of a branch tank engine and a set of four-wheeled coaches which provided a shuttle service between Glossop and Dinting. The development of the Class F1 2-4-2Ts in the late 19th century, resulted in the allocation of several to the shed at Gorton from where two were rostered on to the Glossop branch. Things had changed following the opening of the triangular junction, and no longer was the branch service a mere shuttle between terminus and junction. True, some workings were of this nature, but two other types of diagram had evolved. The first was a Manchester-Glossop-Hadfield service, which involved trains to Hadfield calling at Glossop on at least one leg of their journey if not both. By using both legs of the triangular junction this considerably simplified the operation, as well as providing a service for residents in Hadfield to get to Glossop, their traditional market town. The other development was the diversion of some Manchester-Sheffield trains to call at Glossop. Leaving Manchester London Road, a main line train booked to call at Glossop would depart tender-first, on arriving at the branch terminus the engine would run round its train and then set off smokebox first for Sheffield. On the opposite leg it would arrive from Sheffield running the 'right way', but complete its journey into Manchester heading tender-first. A problem was noticed in the run round, which required very careful driving as there was very little room in the loop for the larger types of engines, such as the Class B7 4-6-0s.

The six-wheeled stock working the branch line services was mostly gas-lit well into the 1930s, so coupled with the 'F1' and 'F2' tanks, the whole scene had a very antiquated look about it. However, with the Depression of this period, many of the local cotton mills began to close and a shift in traffic trends began to appear. No longer was Glossop traffic of a peculiarly local nature, for a new type of passenger — the commuter — was beginning to appear. Forced to seek work in the Greater Manchester area, they took to the train as a means of travel and so new diagrams and workings emerged. As time progressed many of the manual grades reverted back to local employment, but now a new generation of commuter had emerged — the white collar worker. In addition to this, many middle class residents of Manchester began to move out to the fringe of the Peak District, settling in the area

Left:
Though the Woodhead line and Glossop branch had been electrified in 1954, you would be mistaken in thinking that steam locomotives had been banned from the route. That restriction applied only to Woodhead Tunnel, where steam was banned due to the type of concrete used in the tunnel's construction and because of ventilation difficulties. On 2 March 1964 No 43929 crosses Dinting Arches having operated a special LCGB 'last train' along the Waterside branch (opened in 1874). The branch was two miles in length and diverged from the main line at Old Dinting station, on the Manchester side of the viaduct, then descended on a ruling gradient of 1 in 40 to Waterside Mill near Hadfield. *John Clarke*

around Glossop and stimulating its growth. These were the managers, solicitors, office workers and so on, who gave sustained growth to the Glossop service. Improvements were commensurate with the growth in traffic, and the advent of the Class C13 4-4-2Ts and better coaching stock reflected this. Even goods services saw an improvement, with a Class J11 'Pom-Pom' being allocated to Dinting shed. This also worked at least two passenger diagrams, including a 5.25am Dinting-Glossop trip that carried far more bundles of morning newspapers than it ever did passengers.

One of the best services of this time, a Class C13 and bogie stock rostered working, was the 5.17pm from London Road. Known as the 'Glossop Express' it reached the terminus in just 26min, always packed to the gunwales with commuter traffic. On 15 December 1931 push-and-pull working was introduced on some branch services, with 'F1' class No 5729 being specially fitted for the task of motor-train operation. The lightly patronised off-peak trains benefited from the operation and, by the elimination of running round at Dinting and Glossop, timings were improved. At peak times extra coaches were added to the push-and-pull, making the normal two-car formation into four or even five-car set. The introduction of this train gave a far superior ride, for the rear coach of the normal two-car set was a 12-wheel vehicle with a large roomy interior. It is believed that this set continued in use until the outbreak of World War 2, but with the advent of bogie stock displaced from the Marylebone local workings experienced a small revolution which was intended as an interim measure until the electrification scheme was developed. Of course, that was abandoned because of the war, and during this time Class F2s, Nos 5776, 5777 and 5782, and Class C13 Nos 5009, 5193 and 5457 were the branch regulars. Motor-fitted Class F1 No 5594 was kept at Gorton as spare. At any one time two of these tank engines would be allocated to Dinting sub-shed, along with a 'J11' (usually one of Nos 5254, 5327, 6004 or 6045).

The war brought major changes and by the armistice the branch was almost completely the domain of the Class C13 tanks. Most of the main line workings whistled through Dinting but, on Sundays, a Manchester-Cleethorpes working and a few other services did call at Glossop. One of the most stirring memories of these days was the sight of a new Class V2 running into the terminus tender-first, but even this was to be short lived after a revamped electrification scheme was approved at the end of the war. For the unusual requirements of the Hadfield and Glossop suburban services, the LNER envisaged fast, light trains. As these required frequent reversal it precluded the use of locomotive-hauled stock, so the decision was taken

11

to employ multiple-units with driving positions at either end. Consequently, the LNER decided to adapt the design of their three-car Shenfield-London (Liverpool Street) EMUs. However, unlike the single-class Shenfield sets, the Manchester units were to be provided with first-class accommodation for 24 passengers. All the cars were of the open saloon pattern with 174 longitudinal or transverse seats, whilst the doors were electro-pneumatically controlled with passenger permissive control. A single pantograph was fitted to each set, located above the luggage compartment at the driving end of the 60ft-long motor-car. Eight three-car units were constructed and fitted out at Gorton Works and Reddish depot, with the General Electric Co of Witton being the main contractor.

The electric services into Glossop and Hadfield still survive, perhaps remarkably so after the demise of the main line. With the cessation of the 1,500V dc system over Woodhead, the branch was duly converted to the more standard 25kV ac which was employed on the other electrified lines south of Manchester. Further benefits were seen by the introduction of light-weight steel sleepers on the branch in the early part of this decade. These have done much to reduce maintenance costs but, even so, today the stock employed on the branch again has a very antiquated feel about it. As to the future, well this is anyone's guess, but the implementation of a rapid light transit system (such as an extension of Metrolink into Derbyshire) would pay immediate benefits. However, for the moment, the line continues to serve the commuters to Glossop and Hadfield, and is a more permanent reminder of the Great Central Railway than the impotent track-bed of the erstwhile main line which now runs eastwards as a mere footpath, cycle-track and bridleway.

Above:
With the closure of the Woodhead line, the 1,500V dc EMU sets were clearly a dated design and they were scheduled for withdrawal. Although conversion to the 25kV ac system widely used in south Manchester would bring improved availability and reduce operating/maintenance costs, both railwaymen and locals were sad to see the sets go. As the units near their end, M59404M, M59504M and M59604M pass Dinting with the 18.58 Hadfield-Manchester Piccadilly service on 8 July 1983.
Paul D. Shannon

Below:
With the conversion completed and the laying of steel-sleepered track, the Glossop branch saw the introduction of 25kV ac EMUs. The triangular arrangement for the Dinting, Glossop, Hadfield service still remains, but its track layout is considerably simplified. On 26 September 1992 Class 305 No 305516 approaches the single platform at Glossop. Ironically, if the Manchester Metrolink project reaches its full potential then the Glossop branch may undergo a further conversion to form part of the city's light rapid transit system.
Author

2 The Barnsley & Wath Branches

Conception and Construction

The opening of the Sheffield, Ashton-under-Lyne & Manchester Railway to the small town of Penistone on 14 July 1844 may be described as the real genesis of the town. True, it had been an important agricultural centre and market town for many years but, with the coming of the railway, its transformation into an industrial centre began. Proposals to create extensions from Penistone were numerous, with lines to Huddersfield and Barnsley being promoted in the latter part of the 1840s. On 1 July 1850 Penistone began its rôle as an important junction station, with the opening of the Huddersfield & Sheffield Junction Railway. The junction of the line from Huddersfield was some little distance east of the original station, and train services from the H&SJR were faced with an annoying reversal to reach the town's station. Further expansion in the traffic calling at Penistone resulted in growing pressures on the facilities provided by the SA&MR, who had changed their name to the Manchester, Sheffield & Lincolnshire Railway in 1846. However, this company's proposals for a 6¼-mile line to Barnsley were almost moribund from the date of obtaining an Act of Parliament in July 1848. In itself this was a strange situation, for there was a ready and growing market for Yorkshire coals in Manchester and the MS&LR were trying to service this by sending trains from Barnsley to Lancashire via Sheffield.

However, when the Great Northern proposed a westward extension from Barnsley to Manchester, the MS&L were suddenly spurred into action and a further Act for a Barnsley branch was obtained in 1853. Work began shortly afterwards but, from the outset, it was only conceived as a single track with passing places. By May 1855 the work had progressed sufficiently to allow the commencement of a Dodworth-Penistone service and, 12 months later, additional platforms were opened at Penistone to cater for the Barnsley trains. However, it was not until 12 February 1857 that the through goods trains began running. Passenger services did not commence running to Barnsley's Regent Street terminus until 1 December 1859. Coal was the line's main reason for existence, and passenger services

Above:
In 1925 the LNER received the unique Class U1 2-8-0-0-8-2T Beyer-Garratt No 2395 for use over the Wath-Penistone route. Originally numbered 2395, the locomotive became No 9999 under the LNER's renumbering scheme of 1944 and, thus, No 69999 when the railways were Nationalised. It is seen here at Blackwell on 4 May 1949. *H. C. Casserley*

were poorly catered for. This became a continual source of dispute between the L&YR and the MS&LR and the issue was never fully resolved until the line was doubled in 1871. This act finally proved to be the straw that broke the camel's back; the particular camel in question being Penistone station. At last the MS&L were forced to recognise the problem and decided to build a new joint station at the junction of the line from Huddersfield. The contract for this was awarded in July 1871, with the work to be undertaken at a cost of just under £10,000. On the completion of the new station, the MS&LR station was taken over for goods traffic. The new station spurred on the development of the town, which was also assisted by the construction of a new Bessemer steel works on land adjoining the railway.

The huge flow of coal traffic now passing up through Barnsley to Sheffield was so great that it was proving increasingly difficult to provide a path

13

Above:
**Class 76 No 26015 approaches Penistone from the
east on 23 October 1969.** *V. Bamford*

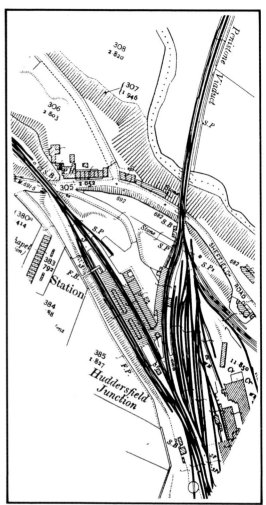

for passenger trains behind the slow moving trains.
As a result the MS&L sought authorisation to build
a second route down to the Yorkshire Coalfield,
with a line to Wath. This line was to become
famous in railway history due to the great Worsbrough Bank, which had a ruling gradient of
1 in 40. This line would leave the Barnsley branch
west of Silkstone and drop rapidly down towards
Wath, where a massive marshalling yard was to be
provided in 1905. The line was devoid of passenger
stations, which is just as well given the interminably slow speeds at which coal trains plodded
up the gradient to Penistone. The advent of this line
finally provided the clearer paths on the Barnsley
branch, which in turn spurred on improved passenger services such as a through Bradford-Doncaster
service. In 1894-95 the station at Penistone was fur-

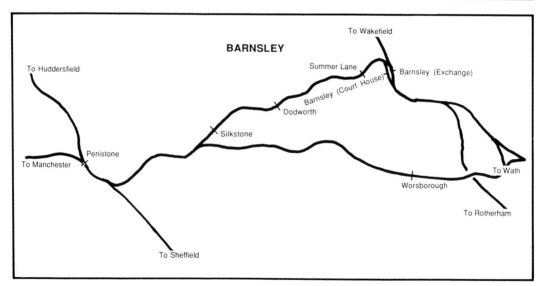

Above:
Coming away from Court House station on 27 June 1959, Class J39 0-6-0 No 64828 heads a Doncaster-Penistone five-coach local. In the bay platform sits a lightweight DMU which has recently arrived from Penistone. The experimental DMU services were to prove a great success, both on the Barnsley-Penistone Huddersfield-Sheffield services. However, they were not introduced between Huddersfield and Penistone until autumn 1959 and it was not until 1983, with the diversion of the Penistone-Sheffield service, that they began to make a regular appearance between Penistone and Barnsley. *Gavin Morrison*

Centre left:
A month earlier the bay at Court House station is occupied by the more normal mode of transport used between Penistone and Barnsley — a Robinson Class J11 0-6-0 with a two-coach train of slam-door compartment stock. This engine was one of Barnsley shed's regular allocation, which were stabled in a rather filthy depot alongside the town's Exchange station. *Gavin Morrison*

Left:
Silkstone was a station with little future in May 1959 despite its regular use by miners going down to work in the pits around Barnsley. More workers used the service to take them up to Penistone, where the David Brown foundry employed large numbers of men. Freight facilities lasted at Silkstone for a further four years, eventually finishing on 1 February 1963. *Gavin Morrison*

ther improved as a result of the MS&L's expansion towards London, and the subsequent change of name to the Great Central Railway.

The Lines Described
Leaving Penistone the line to Barnsley ran for a short distance along the main line before curving away to the northeast at Barnsley Junction. Immediately beyond the junction the line crossed the val-

ley of the River Don by the curved formation of the Oxspring Viaduct, before heading on a falling gradient into the twin bores of Oxspring Tunnel. Having pierced the watershed, the line continues downhill on a 1 in 100 gradient through pretty wooded countryside to eventually pass West Silkstone Junction where the Wath line diverged. Silkstone station followed next, serving an attractive village to the west of Barnsley. More wooded countryside is encountered and, apart from the occasional clue, there is little evidence today to suggest that this was part of the great Yorkshire coalfield. However, the geography changes suddenly and dramatically as the railway curves into Dodworth, where a huge mine complex once dominated the scene. You could always tell you were there, even in the dark, for the train suddenly slowed to a little more than 20mph as a speed restriction was imposed on a section of the line where the colliery sidings met the branch. Summer Lane was the next station, situated on a downward gradient of 1 in 67 after the branch had made a short climb for the first time since leaving Penistone. From here the line took on a suburban feel as it steepened to 1 in 50, eventually coming in sight of the L&YR Barnsley-Wakefield line near Mill Lane. A connection was provided with the L&YR line and, after initially using Regent Street station, improvements at what became known as the Exchange station saw the diversion of Penistone trains. However, the L&YR decided to recoup some of its costs and began charging the MS&L exorbitant rates for the privilege of using its single platform station. So, when the Midland route opened to Barnsley in 1870, the MS&LR began sharing the new Court House station with the MR.

I never had the opportunity to travel the Wath branch in its entirety since, being a freight line, the legal opportunities to do so were rather limited. I once rode in the rear cab of a Class 76 travelling light engine, but had the misfortune to get caught and subsequently flung off by an inspector at Worsbrough. Nevertheless, it was an interesting branch, which quickly dropped through pretty countryside after leaving Silkstone West Junction. At Moor End it crossed a substantial embankment, then ploughed through a deep cutting before reaching the East Silkstone Junction where a small branch diverged to serve a neighbouring colliery. On the opposite side of the junction imposing views could be obtained across the valley to Wentworth Castle. Passing south of Dodworth another large mine was served, before the line crossed a shallow valley which would eventually carry the M1 motorway. Down through Worsbrough Bridge and on past Worsbrough Dale Goods yard. The line then passed beneath the Midland line into Barnsley, before coming down to a complex triangular junction with the GCR's line from Sheffield to Barnsley. Beyond

Above:
A bit further east along the line, at Dodworth this time, No 67445 waits to recommence its trip up to Penistone. This was the last few weeks of passenger service on the line between Barnsley and Penistone, which would cease on 29 June 1959. The goods depot remained open at Dodworth until 1 June 1960. It was almost 25 years before passenger trains would begin calling at the village once again. *Gavin Morrison*

Below:
Also seen on 9 May 1959 Class C14 4-4-2T No 67445, stands at Summer Lane station. By this time the once numerous class, which had been introduced 52 years earlier, are down to just four remaining examples, with only Nos 67445/7-8/50 remaining. *Gavin Morrison*

here trains could travel in a number of directions, but they were invariably routed into the hump marshalling yard at Wath. This had no less than 15 reception sidings and 110 roads, and had enjoyed the distinction of being the first ever gravity operated marshalling system in this country.

Services and Demise

From the outset it was the powerful little MS&L and later GCR tank engines that enjoyed the branch passenger services up to Penistone. For years these were the almost regular preserve of Class C13 and C14 4-4-2Ts. However, 4-4-0 tender classes were commonly seen on the workings, whilst the Doncaster-Penistone services benefited from an exceptionally diverse variety of motive power. Locomotives being out-shopped from the 'Plant' at Doncaster after refit were often sent to Penistone on 'running-in' turns and evaluation tests, the steep gradients sorting out any problems that had not thus far been identified. One common feature of trains regularly rostered on to the Penistone run was a crescent shaped area where paint was burnt off the smoke-box door, a significant identification of the hard work occasioned in the operation of branch trains. Goods trains were usually handled by GCR 0-6-0s and 0-8-0s, often working double-headed with a banker in the rear. The intermediate stations on the line closed in 1959 with the withdrawal of the Barnsley-Penistone passenger service, although through trains continued to run over the line. When the M1 motorway was built in the 1960s, the railway bridge crossing over the new highway was constructed with a single-track deck, in what was then described as 'a justifiable means of reducing expense'. In some ways it may have been, for the

railway was little used between Dodworth and Barnsley, the bulk of the coal from the pit being consigned to power stations in Lancashire meant that the bulk of the traffic flow was up towards Penistone. A pair of Class 37 diesels usually handled the first part of the working, with transfer to Class 76 electric locomotives taking place at Penistone or (occasionally) Dunford Bridge.

The Wath branch was somewhat different, for it had seen the benefit of massive investment in the immediate postwar period with the Woodhead electrification scheme. With this scheme the work progressed in three sections, but it was the Central Section between Wath and Dunford to which priority was given in every respect. A major problem facing the electrification teams were the effects of mine subsidence in the area, particularly between Wath and West Silkstone Junction. To overcome this difficulty, equipment for supporting the overhead supplies was made adjustable, so that the catenary support arms could be raised or lowered as needs warranted. That this was a very real problem can be evidenced from the fact that one section, between Wath and Worsbrough, sank by almost three feet immediately prior to the commencement of electrified services. The advent of the electric locomotives made one of the country's most powerful engines redundant, after it had served on the line since being introduced by the LNER in 1925. Beyer-Garratt 2-8-8-2 No 2395 was then hauled off to an untimely end at Doncaster, but it left behind a lasting impression on all those who witnessed its slow stately passage up Worsbrough Bank hauling the huge coal trains destined for Dunford Bridge and beyond.

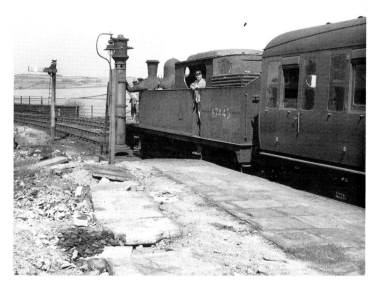

Left:
Having arrived at Penistone, the 'C14' is put into the Huddersfield platform where it takes on water from the old L&YR water column. Today's station uses just this side with the three main line platforms out of use following the closure of the Woodhead route. Beyond the engine will be seen the start of the parapet for Penistone Viaduct, on which is situated a row of railings. These were erected in the 1880s after a drunk passenger got out of an evening arrival from Huddersfield when it was held up by an approach signal. Thinking he was on the platform the man walked safely along the coping stones, but horrified staff eventually pulled him to safety. *Gavin Morrison*

Beeching left the Woodhead route well alone — he recognised its value as perhaps the most modern line in the country — but, by January 1970, passenger trains had been withdrawn from the route with what seemed indecent haste. Despite this, British Rail promised the line's future was secure and went on to describe it as the most important east-west rail freight route in the country. And we were all gullible enough to believe them! Within a few years Woodhead's 'secured future' as a freight line was in doubt, for BR had suddenly realised they had a surfeit in trans-Pennine routes, and could manage quite well with just two instead of four. However, as three of these routes carried substantial local traffic, Woodhead was the obvious one to close. Two factors influenced this decision, the lack of traffic and the savings involved in closure, supposedly amounting to around £65 million before the end of the century. For example, when Wath Yard opened in 1907-08 it was supplied by over 40 collieries or mines but, by the early 1980s, those it served could be counted on one hand. Thus, BR reduced movements to 25 trains each way per day which meant a lower demand on the Class 76 Bo-Bos, and many were taken out of service and cut up at Gorton. In any case the '76s' were almost life-expired, and certainly under-powered for the 30 wagons making up a modern coal train. To handle one of these up to Woodhead, two Class 76 locomotives were required at the head of the train, whilst two more were required for banking at Worsbrough. Despite the most concerted effort ever launched to save a freight line, Woodhead and the Wath branch closed to traffic on 20 July 1981; the unbelievable had happened.

Yet out of all this darkness there did come a little light, although even that emerged in a cloud of gloom. The South Yorkshire and West Yorkshire PTEs, who had argued for years about the future and viability of the Huddersfield-Penistone-Sheffield service, finally came to head-on conflict. South Yorkshire said it would not support the service to Penistone, West Yorkshire retorted that a line from Huddersfield to Denby Dale (the last station in West Yorkshire) would not be worth retaining in isolation. The wrangling went on, but then someone came up with the bright idea of rerouting the trains via Barnsley. This would achieve the removal of all trains over the Woodhead route (except those running up to the Stocksmoor Works of British Steel). It would provide a useful Penistone-Barnsley service as well as still linking Huddersfield and Penistone to Sheffield, it seemed immaterial that the journey times would be increased substantially. In 1961 I used to catch the 7.40am train from Huddersfield to Sheffield on a regular basis, it was sometimes a little late in arriving at Victoria station, but usually it arrived dead on time at 8.36am. Today a train still leaves Huddersfield around the same time (7.39am to be precise), and in these days of high-speed travel it pulls into the city's Midland station at 9.06am — and they call that progress. Fortunately the diversion via Barnsley has seen the reopening of stations at Silkstone Common and Dodworth, although they are basic affairs with little more than bus shelter-type waiting areas. Still one must not grumble, they might just as well have taken it into their heads to pull the whole lot up.

3 The Clayton West Branch

Conception and Construction

Ostensibly, the Clayton West branch was promoted to capture traffic from a small coal mining and textile town in the Dearne Valley. However, its origins are clearly rooted in railway politics and protectionism; for the primary reason behind its projection was to prevent other railway companies building a route between Huddersfield and Barnsley. The construction of the Huddersfield & Sheffield Junction Railway in 1850 had opened an artery between what is now West and South Yorkshire and, at the time of promotion, there had been a genuine desire to provide a branch from this line through the Dearne Valley to Barnsley. However, with the opening of the L&YR's branch from Horbury to Barnsley (also in 1850) the company had already managed to tap the lucrative colliery traffic in that area. Two other routes were available to take the South Yorkshire coal traffic west to Lancashire, one of which was discussed in the previous chapter, the other struck through the Dearne Valley to the southeast of Huddersfield. As will be seen in Chapter six, the Midland, Hull & Barnsley and the LNWR all had an eye to taking a line via the Dearne and Kirkburton valleys. The L&YR were

obviously concerned about this threat to their traffic, so protectionism was introduced.

The H&SJR's Darfield branch proposals had been drawn up by Alfred S. Jee in 1845, who proposed a 15¾-mile long line from Shepley which would have involved two tunnels (440yd and 1,320yd in length) and a 78ft high viaduct. This scheme was rejected at the committee stage in Parliament, but it raised hopes in the locality which were to continue for the next half century. By 1865 the Midland and LNWR were actively promoting

Below:
Prior to World War 1, all the siding accommodation for the junction was on the branch itself, with just a single trailing siding from the main line on the northwest side. The more extensive siding accommodation, situated on either side of the running lines, dated from 1917 after the provision of a large-pattern L&YR signalbox. Even so, it is reasonable to assume that the extra width on the first section of the branch may have been provided with exchange sidings in mind. In June 1958 Fowler 2-6-4T No 42410 crosses the junction above Copley Lane, the siding accommodation being clearly evident. *Peter Sunderland*

their through route via Kirkburton, but the Derby-based company was bought off by the L&YR who offered it access to Huddersfield over the H&SJR. Yet the hopes for a line through the Dearne Valley did not die away, and it is very significant that, between the first proposal of 1844 and the Lancashire & Yorkshire Railway's West Riding Branches Act of 1866, there were no less than 28 separate schemes put forward. The small town of Clayton West, some eight miles due southeast of Huddersfield, presented the compromise. It offered a good return of traffic from local woollen mills and collieries, but more importantly a branch to the town would prevent any other intrusion into the area. The branch was to be single but, in view of proposals for an extension to Barnsley, powers were acquired to take extra land should the line require doubling. Costs for the 3½ mile long branch were estimated at £75,000, but contracts were not awarded for some considerable time, thus indicating the L&YR's reluctance to commence the work.

Even though the initial Act specified that the branch must be completed within five years of authorisation (ie by 1871), the first sod was not cut until 27 November 1872. The ceremony was held at Skelmanthorpe, where a large crowd gathered in atrocious conditions to watch the celebrations. The contract was awarded to J. Hall Clark of Warwick, and Thomas Swinburn became resident engineer. Progress on the construction work was terribly slow, so the L&YR repeatedly had to ask Parliament for extensions to the fixed time limit allowed for completion. Some of the worst problems were encountered with the 511yd long Shelley Woodhouse Tunnel, which resulted in the contractor repeatedly asking for more money to cover the extra work. In agreeing to pay additional 'hard rock' payments to the contractor, the L&YR suggested that his task might be easier if a double-track bore were to be built. Undoubtedly the company struck the better bargain, and thereby made provision for a possible extension. In 1877 an Act provided the company with a final time limit of 1 August 1879, but despite all the extra time allowed, the branch only just managed to receive Board of Trade Sanction on 30 July 1879 — two days before the deadline.

During the construction period, proposals for a through line were given substance when a new survey was carried out between Clayton West and Darton in 1872. At an estimated cost of £175,000, this line would have required a 1,936yd long tunnel at Clayton Hall just south of Clayton West station. However, the L&YR appeared content to leave things as they were. Later on further Parliamentary powers were obtained for a joint GNR/L&YR extension but, when the L&YR again failed to follow these powers up, a deputation was sent from

Left:
In November 1959 British Railways introduced DMUs on to the branch. These proved to be an immediate success and thereby revitalised traffic, as illustrated by this view, on 4 April 1964. There were the occasional failures, however, and in one incident a 'WD' 2-8-0 had to be sent from shunting Park Mill Colliery Yard to recover a unit that had failed at Skelmanthorpe. The unit was carrying school-children home from Honley, and they thought it great sport to be towed down the bank to the terminus at Clayton West. *Royal Commission For Historic Monuments*

Left:
Colliery traffic was always quite substantial and the Park Mill screens, adjacent to the terminus, generated extensive levels of traffic over the years. On 22 May 1979 NCB Hudswell Clark 0-4-0DM No D1094, originally from Grimethorpe Colliery, sits in the sunshine at Park Mill awaiting its next turn of duty. *Adrian J. Booth*

Barnsley. When they arrived at the L&YR's headquarters in Manchester, the railway chairman, George Armitage, commented that the three-mile extension would be too expensive ever to justify its construction so the powers were allowed to lapse in 1899. Final hopes of an extension were pinned on the passing of the Light Railway Act, which meant that a less expensive scheme could be submitted to Parliament. On 22 September 1906 the nominally independent Clayton West & Darton Light Railway Act gained Royal Assent, but lack of finance and the intervention of World War 1 finally killed off the scheme.

The Line Described

From the junction the line headed northeast past the delightfully named Ozzings Ings Farm running along a substantial embankment to the portal of Shelley Woodhouse Tunnel. Interestingly the portal at the east end was one of the first structures in the country to benefit from the new Marshalite simulated sandstone block, when refurbishment was required shortly after nationalisation. On emerging from the tunnel and its associated entry cutting, the line turned due east towards Skelmanthorpe. A short distance further on a lay-back siding was provided on the south side of the line, and in this siding the Royal Train, carrying HRH Princess Elizabeth, was stabled just prior to her Coronation as the Queen. The branch just had one intermediate station, Skelmanthorpe, where Emley Moor Colliery provided substantial coal traffic. A deep cutting was encountered beyond the station. After Skelmanthorpe the line ran downhill to Clayton West along an almost continuous embankment. At the terminus a single platform with a release road was provided, whilst an attractive stone station and a glass/iron canopy were provided for passenger comforts. Another colliery belonging to Messrs Stringer & Jaggar, Park Mill, was found at Clayton

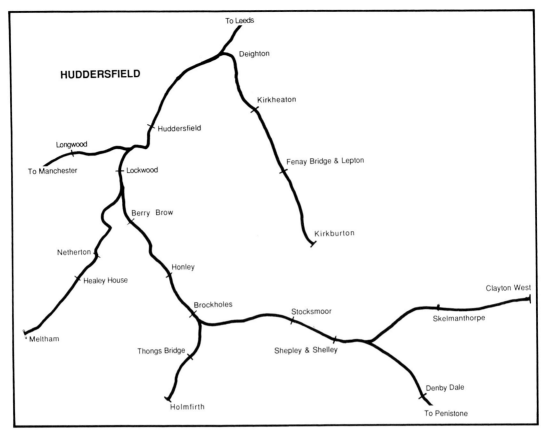

HUDDERSFIELD

To Leeds
Deighton
Kirkheaton
Huddersfield
Longwood
To Manchester
Lockwood
Fenay Bridge & Lepton
Berry Brow
Netherton
Honley
Kirkburton
Healey House
Brockholes
Stocksmoor
Clayton West
Skelmanthorpe
Meltham
Thongs Bridge
Shepley & Shelley
Denby Dale
Holmfirth
To Penistone

Below:
The other main colliery in the area, Emley Moor, was located directly adjacent to the intermediate station at Skelmanthorpe. A variety of locomotives worked the colliery screens and sidings. Alongside the long list of steam engines were two Fowler 0-4-0DM locomotives of 1939 vintage. Fitted with an 80hp 6A engine one of these remained at work until the early 1970s, when it was relegated to stand-by duties. Seen on 2 July 1978 it is out of service, awaiting disposal. *Adrian J. Booth*

West and its screens were immediately adjacent to the goods yard. These were served by a fan of sidings radiating off the branch and whilst they were worked by L&YR and LMS locomotives, they were not maintained or provided by the railway company.

Services and Demise
Initially passenger services along the branch were quite unusual, in that coaches for Clayton West were 'slipped' from Holmfirth or Penistone trains at Brockholes. A Barton Wright 0-6-2T stabled (in the open) at Clayton West Junction, worked these trains as well as doing the shunting along the branch. The engine was shedded at Mirfield and would go back for a wash-out and general maintenance each Saturday evening, returning up the branch on the wagon empty working that left Mirfield Yard early on a Monday morning. In later years the slip workings were discontinued, following several accidents, and Aspinall 2-4-2Ts worked services from Clayton West through Huddersfield to Bradford or Halifax. Coal traffic was always the main feature of the branch, though passenger services were reasonably well patronised — including those trains which carried local school children to

the grammar school adjacent to the H&SJR line at Honley. Passenger services benefited from the introduction of DMUs on 2 November 1959, though steam remained in use on excursion and freight trains down to the summer of 1968. Skelmanthorpe closed to goods traffic on 1 June 1964, but a private delivery siding remained to serve Emley Moor Colliery. On 9 October 1966, the station was reduced to an unstaffed halt and later the wooden buildings were demolished leaving just a small part of the original structure as an open-fronted shelter. Clayton West remained open to goods traffic until September 1970, but thereafter the yard was retained as a private siding for Park Mill Colliery. Unlike the other branches off the Huddersfield-Penistone line — to Holmfirth and Meltham — the Clayton West branch was to survive the Beeching closures. The line's finances were assisted by the continued heavy coal traffic from the two collieries. In later years, the branch was subsidised by West Yorkshire County Council. However, with the declining fortunes of the coal industry and the uncertainty over the future of the 'main' line, the branch was to close completely on 24 January 1983.

Rebirth

The track was lifted in 1986, but the line's remarkable history had not ended yet. For a local man, Brian Taylor, the head of a small engineering company, saw in the abandoned trackbed the potential for a new miniature railway. At that time he was already operating a narrow gauge 'park' railway in Halifax, whilst his firm was constructing components for a variety of other narrow gauge railway operators. To operate the new venture, Mr Taylor

Above:
Another of the Emley Moor Colliery locomotives, probably Standback No 2, is captured in this view as Type 4 diesel No D392 from Mirfield shunts Skelmanthorpe Yard on 8 February 1967. The Class 40s were regularly in evidence on this work in the mid 1960s until well into the late 1970s but, right up to the end of steam, it was possible to observe 'WD' 2-8-0s working on branch coal trains.
Gavin Morrison

Below:
Branch passenger services slowly diminished and passenger numbers grew less and less, a problem that was compounded by the opening of a new school at Shelley which saw a transference of scholars from the trains. On 26 January 1978 the 12.10 Huddersfield-Clayton West service prepares to depart from Huddersfield's platform No 1, the handful of passengers on board bear mute witness to the fact that the end is near. *R. E. Ruffell*

constructed two 15in gauge steam engines at Shepley, and has subsequently built a diesel locomotive at Clayton West. Leasing the trackbed from the local council, the Kirklees Light Railway slowly extended its 15in track from Clayton West, fighting almost every bureaucratic obstacle imaginable. On 22 February 1989 a Light Railway Order was applied for, but two years hard work still lay ahead. The Order was finally made by Maj Peter Olver on 27 September 1991, with the first train running to a new halt near Scissett which was aptly named Cuckoo's Halt. Life in its first two years was not easy for the company, with the recession of that period reducing expected visitor numbers. One major set back during 1992 was the deliberate and senseless destruction, by fire, of the signalbox at Clayton West Junction. The railway had hoped to remove this to the opposite side of the H&SJR line, making it part of their projected interchange station. However, the local authority granted planning permission for the box to be turned into a private dwelling inside a 'green belt'; despite considerable opposition from the railway preservation movement, local residents and wildlife conservationists. The resulting controversy led to great ill-feeling in the locality, which culminated in an arson attack on the box. Meanwhile work progressed steadily on the KLR, and on Boxing Day 1992 the line up to Skelmanthorpe was opened.

It is eventually intended that the line will be continued up to the former junction, where an interchange will be made with Penistone line services. This would undoubtedly be of immense value to visitors who could reach the miniature railway on standard gauge rail services from both West and South Yorkshire. At the present time great improvements are being made at the once-derelict Clayton West/Park Mill site, with a new road leading to the station with its adjacent boating lake, children's play area and model railway lines. The old goods warehouse is being converted into engineering workshops, with a first floor lecture theatre. Eventually an engine shed is to be constructed next

to the present station buildings, but in the short term a wooden building is planned to serve this rôle at Skelmanthorpe. A 200-space car parking area has been constructed, whilst the remainder of the 5½ acre site is to be developed into an attractive visitor centre. All of this is within a few minutes drive of exits 38/39 on the M1 and close to the M62 trans-Pennine Motorway. The railway is certainly worth travelling to see, for it passes through some beautiful countryside. Located in the South Pennines and close to the Peak District National Park, it is quite close to Holmfirth better known as the location for 'Last of The Summer Wine'.

4 The Holmfirth Branch

Conception and Construction

When the Huddersfield & Sheffield Junction Railway opened on 1 July 1850, it was joined by an associated branch line to Holmfirth. Then a little known woollen manufacturing district, Holmfirth and the surrounding areas were later to become nationally famous as the film location for the BBC Television series 'Last of the Summer Wine'. Though the branch was promoted as part of the H&SJR, it is now recognised that it was the intention to open the line from Huddersfield to Holmfirth in advance of the rest of the line. This would have happened as early as 1848, but delays in completing the main line viaducts at Lockwood and Paddock prevented this. In common with the H&SJR, the contractors for the branch were Messrs Miller, Blackie and Shortridge. In the end it was planned that the line would open on 24 June 1850, but further problems prevented this from occurring. However, after all the early disappointments, the first public passenger train left Holmfirth at 11.25am on 1 July 1850. The opening ceremony was well attended, despite the fact that it was an atrociously wet day. During the first week a total of 1,869 tickets were sold at Holmfirth station, with 674 at the intermediate station of Thongsbridge.

The branch was just 1 mile 28 chains long, but it was always intended to extend the railway to at least Holmbridge — a scheme which received Parliamentary authority in 1847. This extension was costed at only £56,000, but nothing occurred and the powers were allowed to lapse in 1852. In 1873, 1879, 1881 and 1890 further extension proposals

Below:
When the Holmfirth branch opened in 1850, a number of complaints were raised over the timing of trains, missed connections and poor services. Though they were undoubtedly bad, the underlying reason for many of the problems resulted from the fact that the parish church clock was some 15min slow. This fact appears to have escaped most people's attention until a letter appeared in the local paper pointing out the differences between ecclesiastical time and railway time. This was made abundantly clear when passengers reached the junction at Brockholes, pictured here, usually by the fact that their connection had already departed.
Bamforth & Co

Above:

Pulling over Brockholes Junction in June 1958 Fowler 2-6-4T, No 42622 heads a three-coach train from Leeds to Holmfirth. The stock is something of a mixture of LMS types, a difference that is further emphasised by the carmine and cream and maroon liveries. The buffer stop in the foreground marks the end of what were the line's engineering sidings, erected here when this part of the L&YR was divorced from the rest of the system.
Peter Sunderland

Centre right:

It was essential for the branch to run on a shelf along the side of the valley in order for it to have the altitude for the proposed extension on towards Holme Moss. Though the line actually fell on a gradient of 1 in 100 as far as Thongsbridge, the climb of 1 in 120 on the subsequent mile journey up to Holmfirth not only maintained the 504ft (154m) altitude of the junction, but actually took the line to a terminus of 518ft (158m) above sea level. In July 1957 2-6-4T No 42377 reaches the terminus with a three-coach train from Bradford. *Author's collection.*

Right:

At the end of the main waiting room, and before the woollen trans-ship shed, there was a large open waiting area situated beneath the overall canopy. Quite often it was full of parcels and loose goods awaiting consignment by passenger train but, during peak holiday periods, it was kept clear of such traffic and provided with seats. This view dating from the 1940s shows this area and presents an evocative picture of rail travel at that time. An array of attractive posters extol the virtue of picturesque destinations on both the LMS and the LNER, whilst enamelled metal signs promote a variety of wares. *Author's Collection*

were put forward, but on each occasion no progress was made in taking the line beyond Holmfirth. Yet there can be little doubt that the L&YR had intended to extend the line, for it had been built with double track throughout despite its very short length. One of the schemes envisaged the line extending up the Holme Valley before tunnelling below Holme Moss, then connecting with MS&L around Crowden.

The Line Described

From a junction near Brockholes station the line headed almost due south in a gentle curve, crossing the Mytholmbridge Viaduct before reaching the branch line's only intermediate station at Thongsbridge. However, this viaduct was something of a bone of contention with the travelling public when the line opened, as the embankment planned for this point had been replaced by a frail-looking timber trestle. Public confidence in the structure was not helped when it was blown down during the course of construction! Despite various petitions calling for its replacement, the trestle remained in place until 1865. Unable to allay fears any longer the L&YR commissioned a replacement in stone but, as it neared completion, the viaduct collapsed on 3 December 1865 taking the trestle with it. Having discounted the use of a locomotive-hauled passenger train between Holmfirth and the gap, the company introduced a replacement horse-bus passenger service 12 days later. It seemed that the problems would be best resolved by constructing an embankment, a particularly appealing idea in view of the huge quantities of spoil requiring disposal from construction sites on the nearby Meltham branch. However, difficulties in obtaining the necessary land led to the rebuilding of the viaduct. After the completion of the new viaduct the line reopened on 11 March 1867.

Another rebuilding project on the branch was Thongsbridge station. The station was situated in a deep cutting, spanned by overbridges at either end. The original layout had the platforms staggered either side of the bridge at the west end of the cutting. The main buildings being situated on the Huddersfield-bound side, but this arrangement was twice criticised by the Board of Trade after accidents to passengers using the station. So, in 1893, the L&YR let a tender to Robert Leake & Co to build a new down platform opposite the main station buildings and extend the gap between the running lines from 5ft 9in to the standard 6ft. During 1901 the Huddersfield-bound platform was heightened, a new two-storey booking office was constructed and an iron-lattice footbridge erected across the running lines. At the same time the company extended the goods yard (initially just a single loop off the Huddersfield-bound line), by providing sidings on the site of the old down platform. As this meant that the yard was now on both sides of the running lines, a cartway was built to provide access between the two sides. A lifting barrier worked from the signalbox protected the crossing, it being interlocked with signals for the running lines.

Holmfirth station presented a fine picture of a branch line terminus, with mock-gothic buildings and wonderfully ornate chimneys. The first station buildings were all contained in what was later to become the stationmaster's house, situated at the end of the long single platform. Plans in the author's possession show the proposed layout for Holmfirth had the extension gone ahead, with two long platforms and a bay on the down side. However, this extension was not to be and, with the proposed viaduct across the town firmly scotched, the L&YR installed a 45ft diameter loco turntable at the western end of the platform in March 1883.

The original layout at Thongsbridge saw the platforms staggered either side of the overline road bridge carrying Heys Road. A sleeper-built barrow crossing gave access to a long narrow platform serving Holmfirth-bound passengers on the west side of the bridge, which may also have had a set of steps connecting it up on to the bridge. However, as there were never very many people willing to pay the 1d (0.4p) for the short journey into Holmfirth, this platform was usually only used in any numbers by people arriving from the south. Accordingly it was devoid of all but the most basic facilities, though, just beyond the west end of the platform, was the signalbox of 1880 that was installed by the Gloucester Wagon Co. *B. C. Lane Collection*

When the station was rebuilt for the L&YR by Robert Leake & Co in 1901-2, the opportunity was taken to resite the down platform opposite the original one. The cutting was considerably widened and the clearance between the track was improved to the standard 6ft. Again, only a basic waiting room was provided on the down side, but a more comprehensive set of facilities were to be found on the up side. A flight of steps led up from the platform to the booking hall which was located on the upper floor of a two-storey building. This, in turn, led directly out on to Heys Road. A footbridge from the booking office spanned the tracks and steps led on to the down platform, as shown in this June 1958 picture. *Peter Sunderland*

This was the first stage in a variety of improvements during the latter part of the 19th century. It was followed in 1887 by several changes in the goods yard. In 1890 the goods office was transferred from the passenger station buildings, when the vacated room was 'acquired' by the stationmaster as his office. The platforms were extended to accommodate the longer trains using the station, whilst their height was raised to meet the newer coaching stock being used on the service. A product of these changes saw the bay platform being filled in, and new waiting rooms being erected between the old station buildings and the woollen piece warehouse. However, perhaps the most significant improvement was the addition of an overall glass and iron canopy 180ft long. Another 'improvement' of the era saw the erection of a new signalbox, after the old one was destroyed by a serious fire in 1899.

Services and Demise

The line was always very well patronised, with passenger trains regularly consisting of three or more carriages. On Tuesdays (half-day closing), cheap day tickets were issued to Huddersfield and Halifax necessitating the addition of an extra coach to the 12.40pm train. Trains were often so busy that ticket collectors boarded evening trains at Thongsbridge in order to relieve congestion at the Holmfirth ticket barrier. Even World War 1, with its massive cutbacks in locomotive and staff, failed to reduce demand for travel. When a through service to Huddersfield was replaced by a Holmfirth-Brockholes shuttle, the traffic increased rather than declined and the L&YR were forced to reintroduce some through trains. During this period two small hospitals in the area were used for the treatment of wounded soldiers, and it is known that at least three ambulance trains visited the branch — one of them drawn by a Great Central 4-4-0 locomotive.

Most of the passenger trains were handled by L&YR 0-4-4Ts and 0-6-2Ts until around 1900 when the introduction of the Aspinall 2-4-2Ts saw a great improvement to branch services. Freight traffic during the early part of the 20th century was mostly handled by L&YR 'A' class 0-6-0s and 0-8-0s, the principal traffic being coal in and woollen goods out. Goods trains usually ran to Lockwood, Mirfield, Wakefield or Low Moor, but there were regular workings to Aintree, Fleetwood, Goole and Rose Grove. One interesting working of the late 19th century was the 9.30am passenger service, which was extended beyond Sowerby Bridge, providing a through train to Blackpool Central; during the summer months other trains (mostly Saturday services) were similarly extended. Excursion trains to and from Holmfirth were always popular, but one suspects the sightseeing trains that arrived to bring ghoulish spectators to the devastated town after the Bilberry Reservoir collapsed in 1852 were not greatly appreciated. On outward excursions the mill workers from Holmfirth seemed to have a healthy appetite, for when one of these arrived at Penistone for an evening excursion — all the pubs in the town were drunk dry.

The station turntable remained in service until the autumn of 1938, but by now the use of Fowler 2-6-4Ts was causing serious deterioration to its cross beams and bearings. It was therefore taken out of service and replaced by a simple run-round. Thereafter the majority of trains worked tender-first to Holmfirth, smokebox back. The first sign of declining traffic was the closure of the woollen piece warehouse, which saw little use after the end of World War 2. As bus competition increased, passenger receipts began to contract rapidly and closure was announced for 31 October 1959. Steam locomotives operated passenger services right up to the last day, when 2-6-4Ts Nos 42116 and 42413 were in charge of the last trains. In many ways it is a great shame that DMUs, which were introduced to the Penistone and Clayton West lines the following Monday, were never given a fair trial on the branch. If they had been, it is reasonable to assume that the lower operating costs could have helped the retention of a Holmfirth service, which would undoubtedly be well used now in view of the town's growing rôle as a popular 'tourist attraction'. However, after closure to passengers, at least three DMUs travelled the line including an RCTS special in September 1964 and a school special in March 1965 which took the author and a number of his fellow class-mates to Wakefield where the party connected with an educational 'special' to London. The party returned four days later, and this probably formed the last passenger working of the line. On 5 April 1965 the branch was finally closed, but towards the end of the month Type 4 diesel No D259 ran trials along the branch and sidings at Holmfirth before '8F' No 48305 hauled away the last few remaining empty wagons. The line was dismantled in 1966 and for many years the station at Holmfirth stood a derelict eyesore. Ultimately, a firm of property developers moved in and quickly swept away the booking office-waiting room block. In recent years the stationmaster's house has been made habitable once again, whilst the booking office site was subsequently sold to the local congregation of Jehovah's Witnesses. In just one weekend, in August 1985, an army of 2,500 volunteers came to Holmfirth from all over the country, when they remarkably erected a modern stone-built church on the site. Work commenced on the Friday afternoon, and was sufficiently complete to allow building inspectors to grant permission for a service to be held in the 'Kingdom Hall' at 1.30pm on the Sunday.

Top:
The mock-Tudor station house at Holmfirth shown with its superb chimney stacks, which were the station's most attractive feature. Pictured from outside the New Mill road, the 'back' of the buildings are clearly seen, with the 1896-97 buildings nearest the camera. Note the large entrance door in the main building, which was bricked up and provided with a smaller door when the station improvements were instituted. Its replacement entrance is seen just above the Citroen 15CV with the large LYR letters carved in stone above. *A. H. A. Bastable*

Above:
Forty years on the old station still stands, its chimneys still a magnificent feature for those who would look skyward. The hotel at the far end of the station has long since gone, its site now up for sale as a residential building plot. The 1896 buildings, demolished by a property developer in the early 1980s, now provides the site for the local Kingdom Hall of Jehovah's Witnesses. The former turntable well is just visible on the ground, roughly to the side of the first 'for sale' sign seen in this picture. However, the old lamp hut and oil store, which was in fact the remains of an old three-compartment L&YR four-wheel coach, that once stood here, has long since been removed. The story goes that this coach had run away one night and was badly damaged after it fell into the turntable pit, so it was hauled out and pressed into use as a store. *Author*

5 The Meltham Branch

Conception and Construction

The Meltham branch was, chronologically, the second branch to be built from the Huddersfield & Sheffield Junction Railway and was the closest of the three ex-L&YR branches to Huddersfield. It left the main line at Lockwood and headed southwest along the Holme Valley, before leaving this valley by a tunnel at Butternab. Beyond this it joined a tributary valley of the River Holme, not far from the hamlet of Armitage Bridge. Out of all the branch lines in this book, the 3½-mile Meltham branch must be considered as the one that was the most difficult to build. In itself this is quite some claim, considering that all the railways in the area were built through very rugged countryside. Yet, on the relatively short branch we are now considering, there were two major tunnels, numerous bridges, embankments, cuttings and retaining walls of considerable size. Add to this the shortest tunnel on the L&YR system, a station that only lasted a month and a private halt, then its unique character begins to emerge. On top of which, this branch is where your author grew up and 'cadged' his first illicit cab and brakevan rides.

Construction was found to be difficult from the outset, for the surveyors' report failed to discover beds of treacherous shale and sandstone along the course of the projected route. In addition, the surrounding ground was also very difficult, with copious fresh-water springs issuing from the hillsides. This combination of shale and large amounts of water presented the engineers with a most unstable surface on which to work, so landslips were to become commonplace occurrences. Parliamentary authority to construct the line had been obtained on 7 June 1861, when the Meltham branch was incorporated in the Dewsbury, etc, Branches Act. However, the L&YR did not commence work on the line straight away and it wasn't until 1864 that tenders were issued for the construction. A contract was let in February 1865 to Barnes, Beckett & Co of Audenshaw, for £62,718 17s 7d, to include stations, buildings and other works. Richard Armitage & Co, of Huddersfield, was to supply the iron bridges at a cost of £2,400. The first sod was cut on 4 April 1864, by local industrialist Charles Brook Jun, using a silver spade presented by a Netherton mill-owner.

Not all the businessmen in the area welcomed the coming of the railway. Fierce opposition, for example, was shown by Bentley Shaw Esq. His home, Woodfield House, stood alongside the course of the

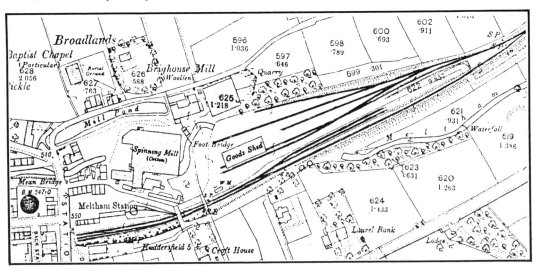

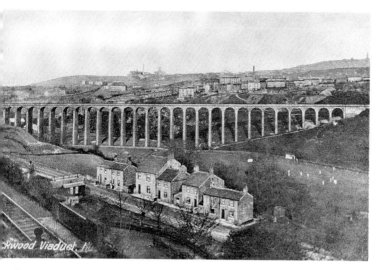

Left:
The Meltham branch is pictured passing through Dungeon Wood, the scene of so many of the geological problems encountered during construction. Evidence of the amount of spoil removed can be seen just below the left-hand (or north) end of the viaduct. Landslips at this point were so severe that they continually threatened to block the River Holme, as well as destroying a row of cottages. Four of the buildings pictured in the centre of this view had to be built by the L&YR as compensation. The bridge in the bottom left of the picture carries the railway over the lane leading up to Beaumont Park, whilst the wooden hut above it is a photographers studio, situated there because this was such a popular visitor destination. *Author's Collection*

Left:
On 6 September 1964 an RCTS special traversed a number of branch lines closed to passenger traffic in the Huddersfield district. It was comprised of a three-car Calder Valley set and a two-car Metro Cammell set. In this view the train, crossing Delves Wood Bridge, wends its way towards Netherton Tunnel. The area to the left of the rear unit was covered by a set of eight contractors' sidings during the building of the line, and it was planned that this would later be used as a loading point for sandstone being quarried on nearby Crosland Moor. However, this never materialised. *Peter Sunderland*

Left:
Viewed from Hall Heys cutting, Healey House station can be seen through the tunnel as the camera looks back towards Huddersfield. At 30yd in length, this tunnel was the shortest on the entire L&YR system. However, in reality, it was just a covered span over the cutting which carried the drive leading to the country home from which Healey House takes its name. *David Ibbotson*

line and, in an attempt to protect its visual amenities, he tried every conceivable trick to prevent the construction going ahead. In 1861, he so incensed local supporters of the line that a public meeting was called at the Oddfellows Hall, Netherton; where it was resolved that 'no local resident would buy ale, beer, or porter, produced at Mr. Shaw's Lockwood brewery, until such times as trains ran to Meltham'. There is no record to show how successful the boycott was! Shaw continued his opposition to the construction and, in his opposition, he was aided by the fact that his house was located very close to where the worst geological problems were experienced during construction. Prior to the passing of the Act Shaw had endeavoured to have it amended and then, following a landslide at Dungeon Wood in March 1868, he obtained an injunction against the L&YR. This prohibited the contractors blasting in case such action might damage his property. Then, for good measure, he sent his family away to safety in Harrogate charging their expenses to the railway.

Woodfield and nearby Dungeon Wood were both problem areas, because the shale found there quickly perished on exposure to the air. This resulted in unstable earthworks and major landslips occurred in November 1865 and in January and September 1866. In the latter incident, the turnpike below the railway was so badly dislodged that the bar house and a row of cottages had to be demolished and rebuilt at the L&YR's expense. A further slip in February 1867 was so serious, that it threatened to block the River Holme, which had to be cleared of the debris. Plans to open the line in May were frustrated by the problems, so much so that when the day of the proposed opening arrived over 60 wagon loads of spoil per day were still being removed. However, on 13 May 1867 a contractors' train managed to run all the way from Delf Clough to Meltham. Unfortunately, work was painfully slow through the wet summer and miserable winter. The inclement weather also resulted in the embankments and cuttings having insufficient opportunity to consolidate. This resulted in the serious slippage of land at Woodfield the following March but, blessed with a fine spring, work progressed quickly thereafter. The first goods train ran to Meltham on 8 August 1868, yet inside three weeks another landslip occurred at Woodfield. Therefore on the day when passenger trains were due to start, 1 September, the line had to close completely.

During the course of rectification further major slips occurred at Hall Heys Cutting in December 1868 and, once again, at Dungeon Wood in February 1869. Finally, in a desperate effort to contain the unstable ground, massive earthworks were constructed at the two most troublesome locations. Some of these retaining walls were constructed to a tremendous thickness, the principle one being 102yd long and 60ft high, with a base 14ft thick. Little wonder it was classed as the most substantial of its kind on the L&YR. The line was inspected by Col Yolland in May and June 1869 but, once again, that man Shaw tried to prevent the opening. However, he had played his hand once too often and Yolland, unimpressed, gave sanction for the line to reopen. The first train left Huddersfield with 11 carriages on 5 July 1869. The trip was marked with great celebration and with crowds lining the way to cheer the trains passage. Shaw was offered a ticket on board, but it is not known if he availed himself of it!

The Line Described
After leaving Lockwood, the line passed on a narrow shelf above the River Holme until Woodfield was reached. Here, a station was opened on 1 June 1874. Built of stone, it had the distinction of being the first station in Huddersfield to be fully illuminated by gas lighting. However, receipts were very low, hardly averaging a shilling (5p) per day, so within a month Woodfield station was closed down, never to reopen. In later years, a proposal to provide a halt there to serve nearby Beaumont Park was rejected because of problems with ruling gradients. The line continued on to Netherton station, passing through two tunnels, Butternab (250yd) and Netherton (333yd). Just over half a mile beyond Netherton came the attractive station of Healey House, which featured a tunnel 30yd long — the smallest on the L&YR. After Healey House, the line passed through a deep cutting at Hall Heys, before crossing the turnpike to reach Meltham Mills Halt. Better known as Spink station, the halt was provided for the workers at Jonas Brook's thread mills. Tickets were issued from the mill offices, using equipment supplied by the L&YR. Meltham had two terminal points, one for goods and one for passengers, with the single platform passenger station being at a much higher level than the large goods yard.

Services and Demise
An engine shed was initially provided at Meltham passenger station to house the branch engine, though this only lasted until the late 19th century. After this, engines from Low Moor (Bradford) or Mirfield worked the services. By the end of the 19th century passenger services were usually worked by Aspinall 2-4-2Ts, but Barton Wright 0-6-0s were also commonly seen. The 2-4-2Ts had a long spell in charge of the passenger workings, but one interesting experiment was the use of 4-6-4T No 11114 which was tried in the area during the spring of 1935. Later the new LMS 2-6-4Ts, based at Low Moor and Mirfield, began to make an

appearance and these powerful engines soon began to dominate the passenger workings. The passenger service remained well used up to World War 2, but falling receipts thereafter saw the withdrawal of such services on 23 May 1949. On the last day of the service, Fowler 2-6-4T No 42406 of Low Moor (56F) worked the last train. A unique feature of the occasion was the 'guest of honour', 90-year old Mr Francis Creaser who, as a small boy, had travelled on the first passenger train 82 years earlier.

Freight traffic on the branch was quite considerable, mainly due to a number of large mills near the terminus. A cotton spinning mill was directly adjacent to the station yard, whilst at least 16 woollen mills were located nearby. A silica brick factory was situated on the hillside just above the goods yard, and a private loading dock was provided to serve this — the two being connected by means of a small tramway up the hillside. At nearby Meltham Mills a large factory complex made up the

Above:
A tractor train departs from Meltham carrying over 30 David Brown tractors including '2D' and 'Taskmaster' models. Departing from the 'passenger' branch in 1952, the train passes the remains of the old ground-frame signal cabin which once controlled the points in the passenger station. In the top left of the picture the remains of the old coal staithes can be seen at the point where the retaining wall curves away to the left of the track. The fence at the end of this wall marks the point where the two road staithes ran over the coal chutes, but these closed as early as 1892 after the timbers began to deteriorate. *David Brown Tractors Ltd*

Above right:
Another tractor train, probably destined for Salford Docks, is headed by 'Black 5' No 45101 from Newton Heath shed (26A). Shipments via Salford began in late 1956 following the Suez Crisis and continued right down to the closure of the branch. Other tractor exports went via Hull, Immingham, Liverpool and Cardiff. Halfway along the train will be seen the junction between the goods station and passenger station lines, the train having come down the former passenger branch. The sign board halfway along marks end/commencement of one engine in steam working. *David Brown Tractors Ltd*

cotton thread mills of Jonas Brook & Sons (later United Thread Mills). As a result large quantities of raw cotton, wool and sand went to Meltham as inward goods. Outgoing traffic included woollen, cotton and silk piece goods, millions of bobbins of cotton and countless tons of fire-bricks. Coal was always an endless commodity required in Meltham, though the arrival of the railway led to the closure of the almost worked-out coal mines owned by my family on the moors above the town. As a consequence of their closure my great-grandfather began a haulage company which carted coal from the goods yard down a specially constructed road leading to the factories at Meltham Mills. Quarries in the nearby hills originated a considerable level of sandstone and silica traffic, whilst gunpowder was brought in for blasting purposes. For a short while the disused engine shed at Meltham was used to store the explosives — but the practice was quickly stopped when the railway inspectorate got to hear of it!

The sudden closure of the cotton thread mills in 1934 not only forced the closure of Meltham Mills Halt, but also threatened the existence of both the whole community and the branch line. However, United Thread Mills were able to persuade David Brown of Lockwood to take over the complex and establish a new agricultural tractor factory there.

Above:
After the conversion of the branch to a 'freight only' line, the passenger station became used as a tractor loading facility. The mound installed for loading tractors can be seen in this September 1964 view, when the RCTS special arrived at Meltham. This was the line's last passenger working and, indeed, one of its last trains. Tractor traffic had already begun to be transferred to road haulage, with BR having announced that the line would be closed the following April.
Peter Sunderland

The terms of the sale were unbelievably generous, though the incoming company had to promise to take on any of the existing work-force who wished to remain in employment. Work on producing tractors began in 1939 but, within months, the factory was doing vital war work — including building aircraft and tank gear boxes. During the war years countless hundreds of tanks were sent to Meltham on 'rec-tank' wagons for repair or rectification, many of which were rebuilt in the station goods yard without being unloaded from the vehicles that carried them. One that was unloaded succeeded in driving over the station weigh-bridge and falling through it.

The tractor works provided considerable numbers of block trains right up to the end. Despite David Brown's opposition, closure nevertheless came on 5 April 1965. So, yet again, the railways lost another vital freight customer and, thereafter, tractors were despatched by road. Even so, many will remember this pretty little line for the amazing variety of motive power it saw. These ranged from the ubiquitous 2-4-2 and 2-6-4Ts, through L&YR 'A' class 0-6-0s, Austin 7s, LNWR 'G2s', 'Jubilees', LNER 'B1s', 'Black 5s', '8Fs' and Austerity 2-8-0s, whilst even 'Patriots' and Royal Scots were noted visiting the line on the occasional special.

Above:
Meltham Terminus in April 1993, its once proud and attractive facilities stripped away. This view is a sad comment on an age which found its railway system disposable, an asset squandered, and perhaps one which future generations would have appreciated.
Author

6 The Kirkburton Branch

Conception and Construction

The line to Kirkburton was the only LNWR passenger branch in the Huddersfield area, but it was one of the most circuitous. Diverging from the trans-Pennine route near Deighton, two miles northeast of Huddersfield, the branch curved across the River Colne, before retracing its steps in a giant loop down the southeast side of the valley. The branch was 4¼ miles long, making the total rail distance to Kirkburton almost 6½ miles — a considerable disadvantage when the direct route by road was around the four mile mark. Even then the line never really reached its given objective and terminated nearer to Highburton than Kirkburton, as it was always intended to extend the branch through the Dearne Valley to the South Yorkshire coalfield. Intermediate stations were provided at Deighton, Kirkheaton and Fenay Bridge, though once again these were all some distance from the settlements they purported to serve.

When the Huddersfield & Sheffield Junction Railway was conceived in the 1840s, the promoters had a choice of two possible routes. One of these would have passed through the Kirkburton Valley and, according to the survey, have run right through where my home now stands. However, as a consequence of the H&SJR adopting a route through the Holme Valley (and the L&YR's repeated failure to build a branch from this line to Barnsley), a spate of proposals were put forward for a railway linking the Dearne and Kirkburton valleys during the late 1850s. Unfortunately none of these schemes came to fruition, as both the L&YR and the Midland Railway failed to make any progress into the district. This left the way open for the LNWR, who seized on the Kirkburton branch as the first stage in a plan to reach Barnsley and the coalfield.

The line was authorised by Parliament on 7 June 1861, with construction commencing that autumn. A contractor's siding was laid in at the site of the junction on 17 October 1861 but, immediately beyond this, the line had to span the wide valley of the River Colne. To do this a seven-arch viaduct was constructed from locally-produced bricks, most of the supplies being transported to the site by barge along the Ramsden Canal which passed

Above:
In its ambition to reach Huddersfield, the Midland sponsored the locally promoted Halifax, Huddersfield & Keighley Railway Bill. This was rejected in March 1864 and was followed, in 1865, by a plan to join the LNWR at Kirkburton with a line from Barnsley. All seemed favourable towards the scheme gaining approval but, without giving any reason, the Derby-based company strangely withdrew the Barnsley & Kirkburton proposals. Shortly afterwards the L&YR granted the Midland running powers into Huddersfield over the H&SJR and, by this, it was easy to assume there had been collusion to keep the LNWR out of Barnsley. As a consequence, the line was thereafter destined to live its life as a secondary branch. Stripped of regular passenger services over 30 years earlier, this view shows the last passenger working — an RCTS special in September 1964 — passing through the remains of Deighton station. *Peter Sunderland*

below. By mid-February 1866 all the piers had been built but bad weather had only allowed completion of the first two arches, the centres for which had been removed shortly before Christmas. However, about 2am on Thursday 15 February, two

The passenger service to Kirkburton was always colloquially named 'Burton Dick', and this continued in common use right down to the end. In this early 20th century view, an LNWR 2-4-2T with a train of six four-wheel coaches calls at Kirkheaton as it heads down the branch. Compare the standard wooden station buildings with the more substantial brick-built goods warehouse behind. This site is now almost unrecognisable as a station today, buried as it is below a variety of industrial buildings. *Author's Collection*

police constables on patrol in Deighton heard a deafening noise, which they took to be a boiler exploding at a nearby mill. Arriving at the scene, they found that the two arches had collapsed and the resulting debris had fallen into the canal. Fortunately flooding was averted, after the canal superintendent mustered a force of over 100 men to clear the debris. Despite this setback work was resumed. The viaduct was cleverly constructed on a curve with a radius of 22 chains and, when finished, was quite an impressive piece of engineering. It was laid with double tracks, although these stopped at the south end of the viaduct. Actually, most of the earthworks on the branch were capable of accommodating two sets of rails, at least as far as Waterloo. Thereafter, those sections, which were not built for double track, had at least sufficient land to enable doubling if it were ever needed. To illustrate the rugged nature of the line, we might mention it was furnished with no less than 21 bridges. Despite all the problems caused by the collapsed viaduct and difficult terrain, work progressed steadily with contractors Eckersley & Bailey finishing ahead of schedule in October 1867. Unfortunately, delays in

the construction of the wooden station buildings meant that the line could only be opened to goods traffic.

The Line Described and Extension Proposals

Beyond the viaduct the line turned south hugging the side of the valley, necessitating a number of substantial embankments, cuttings and bridges between Nab Hill and Kirkheaton station. The spoil from these cuttings was dumped on the west side of the line immediately beyond the station, providing a large area which would have been used for a goods marshalling yard had the line been extended. Six chains further on the railway crossed the Wakefield road, still clinging to the side of the hill. Two very deep cuttings, which (between them) necessitated the removal of half a million cubic yards of earth, were situated on either side of Fenay Bridge station. Thereafter the line became easier for a short distance but, near Rowley, a six-arch viaduct was needed to span a deep valley. Further cuttings and embankments took the line to Kirkburton station where massive retaining walls were built to hold back the loose earth.

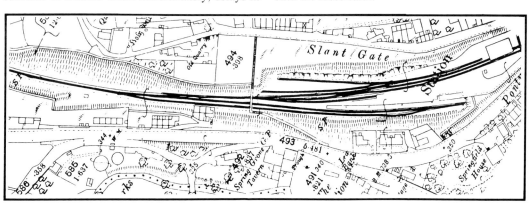

Above:
Another scene unrecognisable today is this view of St Mary's Road with the overline bridge carrying two tracks of railway through Kirkheaton. Pictured in May 1901 for the Kirkheaton Carnival, the bridge is decked out with bunting, union flags, and sprigs of evergreen. Today motorists speed up and down this same section, now much wider, oblivious of the fact that a railway ever crossed here at all.
Author's Collection

Above:
An early view of the terminus at Kirkburton, showing the passenger platform curving into the right of the picture. Had the line ever been extended through to Barnsley, it was planned that the platform would have been moved so that the line could carry on straight ahead and then cross the valley by a four-arch viaduct. The next station up the line would have been the delightfully named Thunder Bridge, which would have been situated at the foot of Dam Hill. *Author's Collection*

At first traffic settled down to a very local pattern, but the objective undoubtedly remained a through route to Barnsley. When the L&YR failed to honour its promise to build a line to Clayton West (with a possible extension to Barnsley), there is little wonder that the Midland began to show more than passive support for the Hull & Barnsley Railway scheme of 1880. This envisaged a line through the Dearne and Kirkburton valleys, promoted in the guise of the Hemsworth, Huddersfield

& Halifax Railway. The Bill for this was approved by Parliament in August 1882, with the Midland obtaining running powers over the projected route in 1883. Sadly this project collapsed in 1886, but only because of the insolvent position of the H&BR. Still seeking to make a connection between Barnsley and Kirkburton, a modified Bill was resubmitted in 1887 though, in reality, all that had changed was the title. As the Hull & North Western Junction Railway, this scheme received Royal

Right:
The first train to Kirkburton contained (amongst others) Mr Baylis for the contractors, Mr Sutton (the LNWR district superintendent) and Mr Buck (the engineer). A series of fog detonators were placed on the track, and the train left Huddersfield to cheering. The weather was wet and cold but, despite this, scores of people turned out all along the route. There was less celebration on 2 May 1959 when 'Standard' 2-6-4T No 80044 arrived at the terminus with its special rail tour, although fog detonators were laid on the track to mark its passing at Rowley Lane, where the last of the old colliery sidings were then being lifted. *Gavin Morrison*

Assent on 5 July. Unfortunately, and despite the apparent backing of three major railway companies, the local company sponsoring the Bill was unable to proceed and the powers lapsed in 1894. Later plans that featured an end-on junction with the Kirkburton branch included the Huddersfield & Midland North West Central Railway.

Services and Demise

In a display of tight-fistedness the LNWR decided that the line would be opened to passengers without ceremony but, to show appreciation for the local population, the contractors arranged a celebration. Around 7am on New Year's Day 1868, the first passenger train left Huddersfield behind 2-4-0 locomotive No 37. At Kirkburton there was a reception by a large crowd, despite the early hour and bad weather. With the failure of the extension proposals being accepted by all concerned, the line settled down to a more mundane future. Initially the passenger trains were well patronised, but a sharp decline in numbers was noted after 26 September 1890 when the steam tram route from Huddersfield to Moldgreen was extended to Waterloo — a situation which became even more pronounced in May 1902 when the tram route was electrified. Though the tram journey times were longer, the fare was cheaper and there were more convenient stops. The scenic values of the branch did not compensate for its poorly-sited stations, most of which were located too far from the communities they tried to serve. In an attempt to compete, the LNWR introduced motor-fitted trains from 1916 onwards using Webb 'Coal Tanks'. Meanwhile no-one could say that the service was inadequate, for, as late as the mid-1920s, the branch enjoyed no less than 12 trains each weekday with an extra mid-day service on a Saturday, there was no Sunday service. Trains took an average of 18min for the down run, though the up journey took from 20 to 26min. In 1921 the seeds of destruction were sown for the passenger service, when Huddersfield Corporation Tramways purchased a fleet of 30-seat single-deck motorbuses

Above left:
When the Kirkburton branch first opened, the station at Huddersfield (for all its magnificent facade) was just one long single platform. Working this presented innumerable difficulties in trying to cater for the LNWR's Leeds-Manchester service and L&YR trains to Halifax, Bradford, Holmfirth and Sheffield. The additional trains from Kirkburton exacerbated the already difficult situation, and the Board of Trade forced a series of improvements to be implemented. Yet, within a century, the local railway network was in rapid decline, and beyond the British Dyes Sidings, the Kirkburton branch was lifted. In 1966 work began on removing the main structures, such as the girder bridge across Wakefield Road at Tandem. A few of us were there to see it go — the author stands in the centre of the group, his back towards the camera as a Zephyr 6 Estate heads towards Huddersfield. *Huddersfield Examiner*

Above:
After April 1965, the only traffic along the branch was destined for the ICI works at Huddersfield. By 1916, when the works were owned by Reid Holliday Ltd, an internal railway had been laid into the works, for which a batch of 45 tank wagons had been ordered from Charles Roberts Ltd at Horbury. The works came under state control in September 1916 and, a decade later, the British Dyes Co became one of the four constituent organisations that made up Imperial Chemical Industries Ltd. Traffic to and from the works was extensive, but it involved a lot of light engine work. One such movement is pictured on 7 September 1968 as a locomotive and guards van pass through the remains of Deighton station. *Gavin Morrison*

to link outlying districts to the tram routes. On 31 October the first of these services began between Moldgreen and Kirkheaton, devastating the branch line passenger receipts. Railway involvement in the local bus scene came on 16 May 1930, when the LMS joined with the Corporation to form the Huddersfield Joint Omnibus Committee. This single act finally killed off the branch passenger service, and the last train ran on Saturday 26 July 1930.

Following the withdrawal of passenger services, freight traffic consisted of a pick-up goods working supported by consigned traffic from the private delivery sidings at British Dyes, Elliot Bricks and several coal mines. As this traffic was still quite substantial, the junction was remodelled for 'goods only' operation on 3 June 1937. However, apart from the trains which ran to the British Dye Works (later ICI Huddersfield), the inward traffic was invariably domestic coal, pit props, and some general merchandise — but not enough to keep the staff in full employment. In the interest of economy the goods depots were all converted to the status of Unstaffed Public Sidings on 1 October 1951. This service lasted until 5 April 1965 when the majority of the branch was closed completely. Track lifting commenced the following year. However, the line remained open as far as the ICI chemical works. This huge 250-acre site had been bought for the establishment of a dye works by Read, Holliday & Son of Bradford in 1915. When production commenced in 1916, the works had come under the control of the Ministry of Munitions, so the plant became part of the newly-formed British Dyes Ltd. A railway system was laid to serve the works, and this eventually extended to over 20 miles of track with upwards of 140 points and crossings, all served from eight reception sidings on the branch. It was a self-contained system with its own team of platelayers, as well as having engine sheds, wagon repair shop, loco cleaning shed and its own breakdown train. Perhaps this is not so surprising when we reveal that the works employed had eight engines and over 300 internal rail vehicles, along with 99 tank wagons and 60 open wagons for main line use. All the engines were 0-4-0Ts with heavy

axle loading. One of them (No 2226) was given to the Keighley & Worth Valley Railway Society for preservation after withdrawal. Even down to the end a minimum of two BR trains a day served the reception sidings, and Sunday working was not unknown. The closure of the ICI railway system finally dealt the death-blow to the last section of the truncated Kirkburton branch on 1 February 1971. However, hope remains that one day the line will be reopened to the works, with ICI recently announcing its desire to begin moving chemicals in and out of the plant by rail.

7 The LNWR Delph and Oldham Branches

Conception and Construction

The LNWR's means of approaching Oldham came not in a direct assault from Manchester, but in a more circuitous way via the Huddersfield & Manchester Railway & Canal Co. That railway had initially been formed as an independent operation to project a line from the M&L main line at Heaton Lodge, to Stalybridge. With support from the SA&MR, this would take a line up through Huddersfield and along the Colne Valley to burrow beneath the Pennines at Standedge. On the western side it emerged into the Tame Valley at Diggle and then turned south, following the western side of the

river, passing through Saddleworth, Uppermill, Greenfield and Mossley before reaching Stalybridge. It was a bold plan, and one with which my great-great-great grandfather was involved with — he had the contract to construct the first single bore tunnel under the mountain. It was, as might be perceived, an expensive line to build, so one of its lesser objectives — a branch to the small village of Delph — was conveniently forgotten by the builders.

By the time the line came to completion the H&M had been absorbed by the LNWR, much to the chagrin of both the SA&MR and the L&YR.

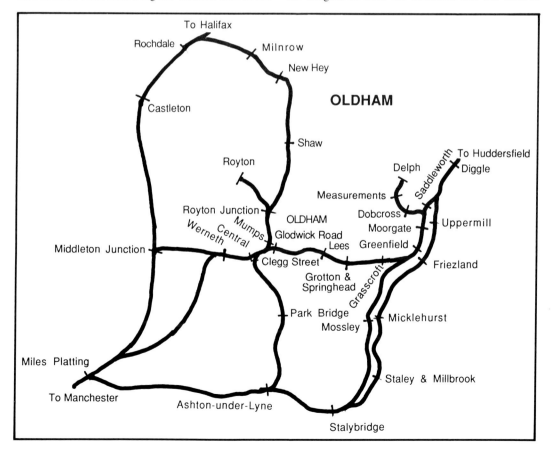

Right:

The idyll of a rural branch line is typified in this view of Measurements Halt on the Delph branch as BR standard Class 2MT 2-6-2T No 84010 propels its train down towards the main line. This was perhaps the autumn of the branch railways, as the face of transport would soon change into a winter of bleak despair. One wonders how much better the service to Delph could have become had DMUs been introduced; the motor-fitted 'Standard' class tanks proved that economies could be made whilst at the same time enticing more people into using the train, what a pity they came too late. *J. Davenport*

Below right:

In contrast to the 'Standard' class, the Fowler 2-6-2T engines were an almost loathed breed; those who drove them on the branch had little to say to compliment them. Seen here at Moorgate Halt, alongside the Standedge main line at Uppermill, No 40056 from Lees shed waits with its two coach train at the timber deck platforms. *J. Davenport*

Bottom right:

Another of the classes to operate on the Oldham-Delph trains were the Ivatt 2-6-2Ts, such as No 41280 illustrated here. Leaving the main line the loco curves away sharply on to the Delph branch in the late summer of 1955. Note the hay-making being carried out in the fields beyond. In the background the small town of Saddleworth, with its fierce Yorkshire patriotism, can be seen — a typical Pennine community, with its rows of terraced houses and mills. *J. Davenport*

Had the SA&MR taken charge it seems likely that the branch would have been built, as no less than four of its directors lived in the upper Tame valley at that time. The development of a line to Delph might have been the furthest thing from the minds of the LNWR's power centres in London and Crewe, but it was pretty important to the folk who lived in the district. Of these a local textile magnate, James Lees, took the lead and hounded the railway company to honour its promises. His doggedness paid off, with the work being finally authorised in the spring of 1850. It wasn't a difficult line to build, not as far as Pennine branches go, and at just 1½ miles and with no intermediate stations it was not to be a taxing proposition. The line was inspected for the Board of Trade by Capt George Wynne in July 1851, and the opening was approved for 1 September. The next stage of the development came in 1856, with the LNWR's branch line from Greenfield to Oldham opening on 4 July. At a little under four miles it was not a long line, but it was an arduous one which involved a steep climb up to the 1,332yd long Lydgate Tunnel. A sharp descent then took the line down through Grotton and Lees to the outskirts of Oldham at Glodwick Road. As the LNWR station was not then completed, the L&YR allowed these trains to use Mumps station until the grandly named (but in reality poor) Victoria station opened nearby.

The Line Described

Beginning our journey at Clegg Street, the 'Wessy' line turned east past the goods yards, complete with their unique curved goods shed and out past Glodwick Road Goods, which stayed open until 1967. Glodwick Road station came next, its ramshackled shell still extant when I made my last trip on the line in March 1964 behind a diverted Sunday stopping train from Manchester Victoria to Huddersfield. Curving round between Moor Hey and Clarksfield, the line passed a private delivery siding serving a local mill. Next came Lees Shed, autho-

rised in 1879, this replaced an inadequate shed at the Oldham terminus and whilst never a glamorous depot it was a hard working one. The sturdy station nearby had the same workman-like appearance but, following closure in 1955, it was just left to decay and fall into ruin. The climb up past the textile village of Springhead, with its huge red-brick mills, took the train into Grotton & Springhead station, beyond which lay Lydgate Tunnel. At the eastern end Grasscroft Halt was to be found, as well as a long curving descent to the main line at Greenfield.

After a sprint up the main line, with its more illustrious forms of motive power, the train swept into Moorgate Halt. From here it ran parallel with the main line, passing Ladcastle Quarry Sidings the branch curved due west just before reaching Saddleworth Viaduct. Leaving the main line behind, the branch clung snugly to the western side of the valley and onto Dobcross Halt, with the Tame-

Below left:
Delph was never what you would call a grand terminus; indeed it was barely functional and, for many years, its passenger operation involved fly-shunting. Alongside adverts for Virol and Palethorpes Pork Sausages (now there's a gastronomic combination!), the two-coach branch set waits behind 2-6-2T No 40059. The push-pull operation might have been the most expedient solution for the branch at the turn of the century but, in a generation that devised the Whittle Jet engine and space rockets, it was hardly to be considered as being a modern means of transport.
J. Davenport

Below:
A salutary lesson in preservation: a scheme that might have developed but didn't. Seen at Delph on 2 September 1973, 0-6-0ST *Brookes No 1* which had been acquired with a view to private operations along the former branch. Several track panels were laid but, in the end, the locomotive, track and a few coaches that had come to Delph were all to vanish quickly. *Gordon Coultas*

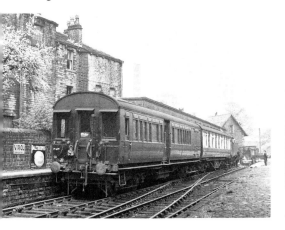

Right:
On the branch from Greenfield to Oldham, BR Standard Class 2MT 2-6-2T No 84015 heads a Clegg Street-Delph train early in April 1955. The push-pull set, having just emerged from the tunnel, has just set down two passengers and picked up one more. Its journey will then take it down to the Greenfield on the main line, where the bulk of its passengers will de-train and await a connection to Huddersfield or beyond.
J. Davenport

bridge Mill Siding immediately adjacent to it. The line then turned northwest and passed under an overbridge before throwing off a siding to Bankfield Mill. Measurements Halt came next, beyond which the branch took a northeasterly course to Delph. Bailey Mill Siding was the prelude to the terminus, its massive form dwarfing the station beyond.

Services and Demise
There has long been controversy about the means of working on the Delph branch in the early years, with opinion being firmly divided between two schools of thought. Some believe it to have been entirely locomotive worked, others feel that services were operated by a horse-drawn Dandy coach. Those who prefer the locomotive theory cite the improbable use of a horse on the main line between the junction, emphasising their claim by the fact that trains on the first day of service were operated by locomotive. Some concede that horses may have been used, but if so it would have only been for a short time. The pro-horse lobby refer to

Capt Wynne's sanction for opening the line, which states in the report 'The Directors anticipate such a small amount of both goods and passenger traffic that they have made arrangements for working the line with horse power. Occasions however may occur to render it necessary to use an engine, and as there is no turntable at Delph, guards have been fitted to the tender of the engine, which may be called into this service, so as to lessen as much as possible any danger that might arise from working the engine tender foremost'.

There are several points to consider in the analysis of this argument and the timing of the trains is certainly one significant feature; this is particularly important, as the timetable does not appear to allow sufficient leeway for such a sedate means of making the return trip from Greenfield to Delph. Yet comparison of timings on other horse-operated passenger services, such as the one to Port Carlisle, does not provide evidence to preclude the possibility on these grounds. Then there is the argument of the sense in taking a horse on the main line, but this does not altogether hold water either. At this time the tunnel at Standedge was still a single-track bore, worked on a pilot and staff principle; so, if the horse-drawn train attained the main line after the passage of a Huddersfield-bound train, it would have ample opportunity of reaching Greenfield before the arrival of a Manchester-bound train. Yet

Left:
By way of a change, this next view illustrates a freight working on the 11am Diggle Sidings-Oldham Glodwick Road freight trip. The vans for this working will have been come from trans-Pennine services and, as will be seen in this view, often included a number of livestock-carrying vehicles. In the charge of ex-L&YR 'A' class 0-6-0 No 52360, the train awaits departure from Lees Sidings.
J. Davenport

there is one other argument, which is little known, that may have some relevance to the issue.

Back in the 1840s, before the coming of the railway one branch of my family operated a successful carting and haulage business between Yorkshire and Lancashire over the Austerlands turnpike. During the building of the first Standedge Tunnel the firm also had the contract for carrying supplies to the navvy camps, and on one of these occasions my great-great grandfather met the daughter of Thomas Nicholson, the main contractor on the project. The couple were married in 1847, two years before Standedge opened in July 1849. On completion of the works, they were able to purchase a number of large (sic) waggons that had been used on the contract and these were then used to increase the size of the haulage business. Despite the advent of the railway, a thriving trade developed between the Holme and Tame valleys, and by now my great-grandfather James Sidell-Lockwood had been born. As a young boy he used to travel everywhere with his father, particularly on his trips over the Pennines. Now one incident from these days was long a source of family-lore, and it may in some way add to the debate. One day great-great grandfather had gone over the Pennines to collect a load of cotton bobbins for the Meltham Spinning Co from Lees, and on his travels he had called in at a railway yard where he was known to the staff. As he was also something of a horse-doctor, they asked him to look at what they called their 'engine' — a large horse named 'Goliath' which was attached to a sort of 'covered waggonette' on railway wheels. As he poked around in the animal's hoof with his pricker he must have touched a tender spot and the horse lashed out with its other foot, catching my ancestor square on the forehead. Thus making a livid scar which adorned an area below his scalp to his death, whenever he was asked how he got the mark, he would reply 'I'm th' only chap as was ivver kicked by a passenger train'. None of this proves the possibility of a horse-drawn service to Delph, serious historians may indeed dismiss it out of hand. There is no way of knowing exactly when this was, or where it actually happened (except that it was between Lees and Holmfirth); or if it was indeed at Delph, how long 'Goliath' pulled the trains up the short branch. Yet, one inescapable fact remains,

Above:
Freight consigned for the Delph branch was usually comprised of coal wagons, and this May 1956 view shows this to good advantage as Fairburn 2-6-4T No 42114 nears Lees as it works the 8.55am trip from Oldham Glodwick Road to Delph. *J. Davenport*

that right down to the very end the service up the branch was always referred to as 'the Delph Donkey'.

The next stage of development came with the Oldham-Greenfield service which in turn resulted in a bay platform being built for the Oldham trains at Greenfield. Two of these workings were extended through to Delph but the other services then operating on the branch, be they horse or locomotive-hauled, were withdrawn. This was a matter of some chagrin to the residents of the upper Tame Valley, and in amongst the campaigners was none other than James Lees. The dispute over services lasted several years, with meetings, memorials and petitions all seeming to fall on deaf ears at Euston. Not only did the services come under criticism, but

so too did the station. By the late 1870s, virtue was rewarded and three extra trains were extended from Oldham to Delph. A little more pressure was brought towards the end of the next decade, when additional services were needed by the local populace which had seen some expansion in the form of a large reservoir construction programme nearby. To carry materials up to the site at Castleshaw, a temporary line (worked by a Peckett 0-6-0ST) was laid in. The station arrangement at the terminus was perhaps the biggest drawback to the provision of extra trains, for due to the lack of a satisfactory engine release, coaches had to be fly-shunted in order for the locomotive to achieve a run-round.

A series of improvements both on the Delph branch and the line to Oldham saw beneficial results in the passenger service, but the Delph line still only had one pick-up goods train each day to serve the massive woollen textile mills in the valley. In 1910 the LNWR railmotor No 5507 was tried, but a series of mechanical faults and a tendency to overheat the passenger accommodation soon led to its withdrawal. Experiments were tried on the branch with a Webb 'Coal Tank' centrally positioned in between two coaches in May 1911, but this early motor train scheme did not last long;

Below:
Not that you would ever know it, but this is the exact grid reference from where the previous picture was taken. The platforms, however, are about 10ft below the surface of the car park. The lattice footbridge seen in the 1955 view would have run where the low brick wall is seen in the middle of this view — indeed if you follow the path that runs alongside this wall today, you will come to the flight of steps that led down from the bridge. The only clue that a railway was once ever here, is the crescent-shaped warehouse in the background. Even though it is listed and protected by the local council, no-one seems to have any real idea what to do with the building so it just continues to crumble as pictured in this October 1992 view.
Author

three days to be precise and it was then back to the drawing board. However, the motor-fitted service was not long in coming and further trials were instituted with another 0-6-2T in November that year. In the following January a full pull-push service was instituted and the line benefited from the provision of new halts. On the branch there was one at Dobcross, another was situated on the main line at Moorgate just south of the junction (though it was only served by branch trains), whilst Grasscroft Halt opened on the Greenfield-Oldham line. In 1932 a further port of call was introduced at Measurements Halt for the benefit of workers at a nearby mill — but trains only called here to coincide with the mill's clocking on and off times, as well as on a Saturday lunchtime.

This set the scene for services down to the end, with pull-push services running from Oldham Clegg Street to Delph. At first it was the 0-6-2 'Coal Tanks', followed by the intensely disliked Fowler 2-6-2Ts, in turn these were supplemented by Ivatt 2-6-2Ts. Eventually, the arrival of BR Standard 2-6-2Ts fitted for push-pull operation heralded a new era. Unfortunately, these locomotives arrived too late to make any lasting impact, though one suspects that the introduction of DMUs might well have saved the branch. It was a well-loved institution and one which still had an extensive service down to its official withdrawal on 2 May 1955. The last train ran on 30 April, an event which was marked with great celebration, a sort of friendly wake for a dear friend. It included a farmer who made a reference to the line's past history, by bringing a donkey down to the station to see off the last train. That train was scheduled to run back empty to Lees, but due to the numbers wishing to travel it went all the way back to Clegg Street. The two lines were not dead yet however, and freight continued down to Delph until 4 November 1963. A moment of brief glory was witnessed on 22 June 1960 when the Royal Train, carrying HM Queen Elizabeth, the Queen Mother, made an overnight stop on the branch whilst *en route* from York to Chester. The Greenfield-Oldham line closed on 10 April 1964, its long usefulness as a diversionary route for the trans-Pennine service deemed no longer essential. Even the once busy service from Bradford and Huddersfield to Stockport, via Oldham, was now a thing of the past. Superfluous in a modern age, the engine shed at Lees saw the departure of its last turn on 11 April 1964, the railmen moved out and the vandals moved in. A private plan to develop a short section of the Delph branch as a preserved line came in the early 1970s, when a 200yd section of track was laid and an ex-CEGB locomotive run upon it. Sadly this failed to develop and in the end proved to be something of a 'dead donkey'.

8 The Oldham-Rochdale Branch

Conception and Construction

One of the most interesting Pennine branch lines is not really a branch line at all, for the railway from Oldham to Rochdale actually forms a large loop off the former Manchester & Leeds main line. However, as its promotion was ostensibly as a branch, it has a rightful place in our account. The original line to Oldham left the M&L near Middleton, headed east up a steep rope-hauled incline, before terminating at Werneth on the west side of the town. In 1847 two tunnels were bored through a ridge of solid rock, so that the line could be extended into a more central location at Mumps. Rope haulage on the incline was probably superseded by the late 1840s, but the 1 in 27 gradient proved a severe obstacle for the free-flow of traffic. As we have seen, in 1856 the LNWR reached Oldham and they were followed by the Oldham Ashton & Guide Bridge Joint Railway in 1861. This railway had been a partnership between the L&YR, LNWR and MS&LR but, when the L&YR dropped out, a new terminus was opened in Clegg Street instead of the envisaged expansion of the station at Mumps. The L&YR met this challenge head on, and opened a station almost immediately adjacent to Clegg Street which it called Central. This may have been an act of petty rivalry or protectionism, but it was to the benefit of passengers who were able to enjoy an easy interchange between the two stations. Similarly, an easy flow of freight traffic was facilitated when a linking spur was laid in just north of Clegg Street.

So long as the OA&GBJR was content with access to Oldham cordial relations existed between the railways, as there seemed to be more than enough traffic for all three companies to take a share. The real difficulties arose when the OA&GBJR expressed their desire to extend the line through to Rochdale and possibly out to Bacup. This was a serious threat, so the L&YR had to act quickly to protect its territory. In reality the rival proposals spurred the L&YR into doing something they should have done years earlier, for they had already surveyed the line but had seen no real necessity to do anything about it. Work commenced in 1861 and, despite the fact that it meandered

Above:

Having got away from Oldham, the first principal port of call on the line to Rochdale was Royton Junction. In the heart of the cotton-spinning countryside, the station was well served by a number of trains — both passenger and freight. In addition to what might be termed as mostly local traffic, the line also saw a variety of special workings heading for more exotic destinations. This was particularly evident during the Oldham Wakes Week, when the mills disgorged thousands of workers on their annual holidays. Most of the workers were conveyed to their destinations by special train, such as this one seen at Royton Junction station behind 2-6-4T No 42653 and Hughes 2-6-0 No 42714. *Richard S. Greenwood*

through Pennine foothills, it was not a very difficult branch to build. Substantial cuttings had to be dug between Higginshaw, New Hey and Milnrow. In all some 170,000cu yd had to be removed between Mumps and Shaw Side alone. The line cost around £348,000 and took two years to complete. However, on inspection the Board of Trade found casting faults in some of the iron bridges required rectification. The work was put in hand and a certificate was issued to allow goods services through to

Rochdale in August 1863. The bridge repairs must have been speedily undertaken, for the passenger services were allowed to commence three months later. The associated 1 mile 20 chain long branch line to Royton opened on 21 March 1864.

The Line Described

Intermediate stations on the line to Rochdale were provided at Royton Junction, Shaw, New Hey, and Milnrow, but there were none on the branch to Royton. Leaving Mumps, once a two platform affair that was converted into an island station at the end of the last century, the line curves due north and crosses the Huddersfield road before passing Lower Moor Goods Yard. As it heads north the line runs through Derker, where a new station was erected in 1987 in order to allow the closure of the inconveniently located Royton Junction station. Presently the line reaches the former Royton Junc-

tion, which had four platforms but no goods facilities. However, on either side of the main running lines an extensive fan of storage sidings was situated. The branch curving away to Royton served an industrial area and thereby does not form part of our narrative, but the line heading north towards Shaw now starts to enter typical Pennine countryside. The cotton industry with its huge red brick mills and gaunt towering chimneys seem less pressing now, but they are still abundantly evident from the carriage window. This was the countryside where the wealthy and influential from Oldham chose to set up their homes and, in Edwardian times, Shaw was reputed to be one of the richest towns in the country due to the number of 'Cotton Barons' who lived there. Up to 1897 Shaw & Crompton station was simply called Shaw. It reverted to this name in 1974 but, following civic pressure, the dual name has now been revived.

Rail traffic to the town is still quite busy today, and a double track exists to a point just north of the station. Beyond Shaw, with its huge cotton warehouse, the line ran on past Shaw North Signal Cabin where a short branch once ran off to serve a small colliery at Bank House. Today the track is now single as it progresses on towards Jubilee but, for the first time since leaving Oldham, the line affords a real glimpse of the Pennines with Crompton Moor seen up to the right. After clattering over the level crossing at Jubilee, the line begins a gentle sweeping curve to the northwest as it swings round to New Hey, where another huge warehouse was once the focal attention of railway activity. The building is still there, large white letters on its side proclaiming it to be a Lancashire & Yorkshire Railway Cotton Warehouse. Sadly trains no longer run in to serve it, instead a profusion of heavy goods vehicles are usually to be seen outside, their loads anything but cotton. A little further on the twin platforms are still extant, but it is only the one on the Oldham side that still has a railway track. The

Right:
Back on the main line, another Wakes Week relief working is pictured as it nears Beal Hey, not far from Shaw & Crompton. The motive power on this run to Blackpool is Newton Heath's solitary Caprotti '5MT', No 44746. Such a scene could hardly be recaptured today; the branch, largely singled and no longer having a north facing spur at Rochdale, has seen no diversion or excursion traffic for many a year.
Richard S. Greenwood

down side platform is now cloaked with a profusion of weeds including rose bay willow herbs and dog roses — pretty in a wild sort of way, but nothing like the immaculate station gardens that once presented such an attractive introduction to the little town.

After New Hey the line loops west through a deep cutting, passes below a concrete monstrosity that calls itself a modern transport artery (the M62 motorway) then runs into Milnrow. Only the up platform is still in use, its modern timber deck and furnishings contrasting with what once stood here. For decades this station has served as a popular destination for day visitors making for the popular Hollingworth Lake about a 1½ miles away; on Bank Holidays trains from Manchester and Oldham were once packed with visitors, picnic baskets in hand and smiles on faces. Today the country park

still attracts a large numbers of visitors, but they mostly come by car — a three-mile round walk from the station proving too much for the modern generation. A slight curve to the west of Milnrow and the branch then runs in a die-straight line, passing through a deep cutting. This is followed by a short tunnel before the railway takes first to an embankment and then a viaduct to cross the Rochdale Canal near Newbold. Beyond here the branch joins the main line north of Rochdale, where a large notice still advises drivers of goods trains to stop and pin down wagon brakes! What goods trains?

Services and Demise
Through services between Rochdale and Manchester, via Oldham, began in the early 1860s. However, the L&YR were forced to run what we would

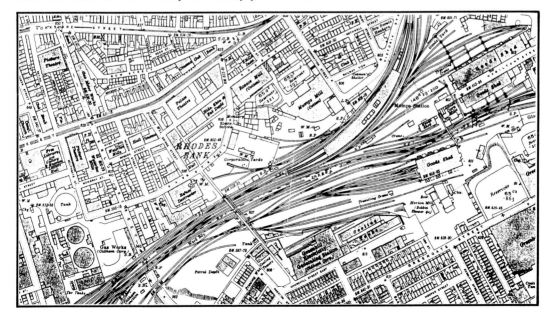

term as lightweight trains due to the severity of the Werneth Incline. A few ex-East Lancashire Railway locomotives were employed on the service, mostly 2-4-0s, but it seems as though it was mostly 2-2-2 and 2-4-0 engines of the Jenkins and Yates types that were used. The difficult incline was obviated in 1880, when a new line was built between Dean Lane and Werneth. Even though this was less severe than the original incline, it was still pretty steep and the operation of an intensified suburban service to Manchester was fraught with problems. The advent of the Aspinall 2-4-2Ts helped, but even these did not have the guts for the job. Something more substantial was needed, and this was provided in the Hoy 2-6-2Ts that were introduced late in 1903. Twenty of the class were built at Horwich to operate the lines to Oldham, Rochdale and Bury — Works numbers 861-880. They managed the traffic well, but they were disliked on a number of counts, not least because they had a tendency to 'spread the rails' in sidings or on tight curves and become derailed. Another fault were the 'watertight' bolts at the front end of the tank which, after a few shunting knocks, were anything but. The water leaked down into the sanding gear, clogging up the system and making life difficult for the crew. When the engines began to develop main-frame problems in c1912-13, the class was relegated to shunting and banking duties. Their replacement on the Oldham lines were the new superheated 2-4-2Ts, which were much better equipped to handle the route than their forerunners had been.

Even so the 2-4-2Ts were not the ideal solution, so the L&YR decided to electrify the Manchester-Oldham-Rochdale line after it had completed its conversion of the Bury line to a third-rail system. Sadly, Oldham missed out due to wartime restrictions. After 1918 a serious lack of resources and finance ensured that steam was retained. Improvements to the motive power situation came with the LMS standard 2-6-4Ts, which remained in charge of almost all local workings until the introduction of DMUs in 1958. Even then the Fowler 2-6-4Ts

Above left:
At Shaw & Crompton station No 49199 works one of the regular Rochdale freight trips. Despite its semi-industrialised nature, the town's station always maintained a well-presented feel about it. Strange to say, this is still so today and, despite being unstaffed, the station presents a reasonably neat face to visitors. *Richard S. Greenwood*

Above right:
Not long before weight restriction and bridge renewals caused the singling of the branch between Shaw and Rochdale, a twin two-car DMU working from Rochdale heads towards Manchester between New Hey and Shaw & Crompton. The date is a wintry 17 March 1979 and, within a few hours of the 14.07 passing this point, the line was to be completely blocked as the snow grew deeper. *Richard S. Greenwood*

Below:
One of only four named 'Black 5s', No 45154 *Lanarkshire Yeomanry* pilots Huddersfield's 2-6-0 'Crab', No 42863, on a diverted express through New Hey. In the background the Pennine foothills begin to climb upwards to the bleak moorlands beyond. *Richard S. Greenwood*

Above:
The ubiquitous No 49199 is seen on yet another local freight trip, this time at Milnrow. Once the goods yard here was packed with vans and wagons, their contents ranging from coal to cotton. Today, little more than a Class 142 is to be seen shuttling past this point as it trundles between Rochdale and Manchester. *Richard S. Greenwood*

Above right:
Rochdale station in its BR heyday — a dirty and grimy edifice — but a well used facility despite its distance from the town centre. In May 1958 Fairburn Class 4MT 2-6-4T No 42284 awaits departure with its train for Manchester, to be followed shortly afterwards by the BR 'Standard' tank alongside. In the near future the line from Oldham to Rochdale could be converted to a Metrolink line, and the route extended into the centre of the town. *J. Davenport*

of Manchester's light rapid transit system, Metrolink, encompasses the branch, it will signal a new era — electrifying a line that might have been so treated over 70 years ago. Unfortunately none of this sees a place for freight, and the once extensive freight traffic which once made Oldham prosperous has either gone or now chokes up an inadequate road system. Likewise the through excursion trains and diverted Leeds-Manchester trains that once came this way with frequent regularity have all but disappeared. Take a trip to Oldham Mumps to see what has happened there, the once massive goods sidings derelict and weed-strewn. To emphasise the shame of it all, a relatively modern signalbox erected to serve the complex is now situated some distance from the surviving sets of rails, typifying and underlying the waste and stupidity of our transport 'planners'.

from Lees shed did not give in gracefully, as they gleefully took delight in substituting for failed diesel services. Some of the failures were quite spectacular, with the early DMUs often giving a superb display of pyrotechnics. Another common failure noted in the sets built by Cravens was that they struggled up the 1 in 50 gradient east of Dean Lane, where one fitter reckoned 'they were knocking themselves to bits'.

Dr Richard Beeching saw the branch as a prime candidate for closure in his proposals for 'modification' in the Oldham area. Had his mad-cap scheme been implemented, the area north of Oldham would have been ravaged. Fortunately his plan was opposed and finally overturned, but a product of this era was the demise of the Royton branch, which was allowed to close in April 1966 along with Central station. What was left was a poor excuse for a railway service, but it provided the basis for the eventual improvements that the Greater Manchester PTE would implement. Though resources have never been sufficient really to develop the line to its full potential, the Oldham-Rochdale link is still there. If the future expansion

Above:
Rochdale today, a shadow of its former self, suffers the malaise affecting many BR stations. One road from the north-end bay has been removed and station staff burn their rubbish in it. Passengers waiting for their trains, such as the one handled by No 142069 to Manchester on 22 April 1992, have to look at such a mess when, once upon a time, neat gardens and hanging baskets adorned the platforms — a time when people were proud of their station. *Author*

9 The Rishworth Branch

Conception and Construction

The Rishworth branch was one of those railways that took an awfully long time in arriving; it finally opened no less than 33 years after its conception. Like the Stainland branch, which we will meet in Chapter 10, the branch was to follow a tributary of the River Calder which carved a deep gorge on the southern side of the main valley. The River Ryburn, which flowed down this valley, was a major spillway for the copious quantities of water that fell on the Pennine hills, so it became eminently suitable for the development of water-powered mills along its banks. It was, of course, the textile industry which predominated, but this was not just limited to woollen goods as silks and cotton were also produced in large quantities. In 1845 the first survey of this rich district was made by the Manchester & Leeds Railway (later L&YR), but due to financial stringencies it was left out of the West Riding Union Railways Act of 1846.

Eighteen years later the matter was again being considered, with plans for a branch of 2 miles 76 chains being drawn up for submission to Parliament in 1865. However, signs of dissension began to appear, with a small faction actively campaigning against the railway. It is interesting to note that in March 1865 photographers, working for the opposing sides, were busy along the proposed route of the railway taking photographs for submission to Parliament. What historic value those views would be today! On 3 April 1865 the case was heard by a court of referees at the House of Commons who, in due course, found for the railway. The *Halifax Guardian* reports the event: 'As on Monday, the decision was expected, the excitement became intense and as the afternoon wore on the inhabitants congregated in the open part of the village (Ripponden), anxiously awaiting the arrival of the all important telegram. At a few minutes to five o'clock a man arrived in breathless haste, having out-run the messenger and communicated the welcome intelligence that the "Ripponden Branch Line Bill" was passed, and in a few minutes after a telegram was received from the House of Commons, confirming the news. The retort spread like wildfire and probably before an hour had elapsed every cottage in the district was startled with the cry of "Hoora, theyn getten t'railwai."'

However, despite all the great celebration, it was still to be another 13 years before the first services would begin. The first delay came in the House of Lords, when once again two prominent local families objected to the proposals, but the railway was found proven and Royal Assent was given on 5 July 1865. However, the 27-gun salute fired in St James' Park simultaneously with the announcement to Parliament was not to celebrate the birth of a tiny Pennine branch line, but was part of a celebration to mark the anniversary of the Queen's Coronation. Two extensions of time had to be

Above:

The junction station for the Rishworth branch, Sowerby Bridge, pictured in the mid-1950s looking from the west end. After arriving with a local working from Wakefield, Aspinall 2-4-2T No 50865 takes on water before going on shed. The scene, apart from livery changes, might have been taken at any time as it captures the dour functional spirit of a well-used urban station. In the far background, just above the engine's dome, will be seen one of Halifax's most famous landmarks, the folly known as 'Wainhouse Tower'. *Kenneth Field*

allowed by Parliament, and it was eight years later when construction actually began. Yet other developments were also noted in this period of inactivity, in that an extension of the line was Authorised to Rishworth, whilst a much grander plan envisaged the continuation of the branch to Littleborough in Lancashire. This would have involved a lengthy tunnel beneath Blackstone Edge, but have had the added advantage of reducing the distance between Leeds and Manchester.

The contract for the construction was awarded to T. J. Waller Esq for the sum of £113,000, whilst Messrs Dransfield, Thomson and Hulme received the contract to build a new station for Sowerby Bridge at the junction of the branch. In 1875 a series of serious landslips, at least one of which had fatal consequences, occurred along the course of the branch due to problems with shale. This led to a proposal to introduce a diversion near Rough Hey but, in the end, this was not necessary. By late August 1876 the new junction station was ready, and it was duly opened to passenger traffic on 1 September. The branch was, however, still some way off being completed and, by now, was nearing £85,000 over the budget. Maj Mandarin inspected the branch for the Board of Trade in July 1878,

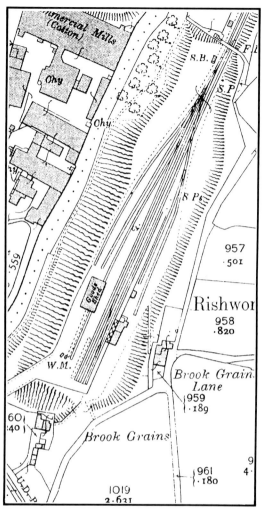

Left:
One of the first obstacles encountered by the Rishworth branch was the ridge of land that lay just south of the junction. This was penetrated by a double-track tunnel which featured ornate castellated entrances. Seen emerging from this bore in c1920 is Hughes railmotor No 1 on a working to Rishworth. *B. C. Lane Collection*

Below left:
It has often been quoted that Kerr Stuart railmotor No 1 worked the Rishworth branch, but there does not seem to be anything to substantiate this claim. For example, no suitable gaps exist in this engine's allocation records which might suggest a period spent east of the Pennines. What probably gave rise to this suggestion is the fact that the trailer carriage from one of the two Kerr Stuarts, was attached to Hughes Rrailmotor No 1. The pairing is captured in this view at Watson's Crossing, with the old coach also bearing the lettering 'No 1'.
B. C. Lane Collection

A further view of the Hughes railmotor No 1, taken at Triangle Station, but this time paired with one of the later batch of trailer cars. Though these units were working a diagram which took them from Rishworth to Halifax, and Halifax to Stainland (and vice-versa) the locomotives were not shedded at Sowerby Bridge. For some reason they were allocated to Low Moor shed, which would necessitate a considerable amount of 'dead' running each week. *B. C. Lane Collection*

An overall view of the station at Ripponden, with a Hughes railmotor arriving at the solitary platform as an 'A' class 0-6-0 stands on the other road. The solid sandstone station buildings and the large warehouse clearly present a significant contrast to some of the branch lines in the area, and might be well compared with Kirkheaton station in chapter six, where the construction was either brick or wood. *B. C. Lane Collection*

when he travelled all the way to the terminus at Rishworth. He was not satisfied with what he saw and ordered seven major areas of work before granting a certificate which would allow commencement of passenger services. On the other hand he did allow, after some modification of the junction points, the commencement of goods traffic from 15 July 1878. Apparently the first truck came from Wakefield, conveying sheep and cattle to a butcher in Ripponden.

The L&YR meanwhile carried out the BoT recommendations, so that on the second investigation it was found 'that passengers services might be commenced'. These actually started on Monday 5 August 1878, when great celebration ensued. The first train left Sowerby Bridge at 8.30am, formed from a tender engine, a guard's van, a composite and two third-class coaches. It is interesting to note that only 35 passengers made the trip. Yet, if the first working was seemingly under patronised, those that followed were anything but. Ripponden only had an initial stock of 1,000 tickets, four of which were sold in advance of the opening. However, by the end of the day, it was estimated that

well over 2,000 people had availed themselves of railway travel — presumably a good half of them did so without tickets! Nevertheless, even when these celebrations were taking place, the goods services were failing to meet local expectations and traders were vociferously complaining about inadequate accommodation and facilities.

The Line Described
Although the line was built as double track, it would appear as though the up line was not used by passenger trains, as the stations were initially built with only a single platform. Incidentally, it should also be mentioned that originally there were no platforms for the branch at Sowerby Bridge. Leaving Sowerby Bridge the line immediately ploughed into the Scar Head Tunnel, emerging at Watson Crossing, where a halt would be erected when railmotor operation began in 1907. Whilst this was of no particular value for local residents, the halt was used extensively by workers going to or from the Watson woollen mill nearby. From here the line ran southwest, on the east side of the valley, presently curving through a large cutting into the station at

Triangle. From here it ran almost due south, passing *en route* Thorpe Mill (the business of F. E. Rawson, the main objector to the railway). A slight twist to the west took it into another deep cutting, before it continued to Ripponden. The station here was also known as Ripponden & Barkisland, and was approached first by an embankment and then a cutting. On the east side of the platform a pair of sidings served the goods yard, with a looped siding running through/alongside the goods shed. Passenger access was via a flight of steps leading to Elland Road. Beyond the station the line crossed over this same road, before heading southwest once again.

The extension from Ripponden to Barkisland was also some time in coming. It did not open until Shrove Tuesday, 1 March 1881. Little is detailed about the reasons for the delay in construction, but all the records seem to suggest that it was a lack of finance rather than interest. The terminus was at the quaintly named hamlet of Slitheroe, but the station was always named Rishworth. As the aim was an extension through the Pennines, it was not a grand terminus, more a glorified wayside halt. Some have called it the smallest terminus on the L&YR and this, whilst not strictly true, might be a very fitting description. The whole terminal area was built on an artificially levelled area between Brook Grains and the River Ryburn, being at a slightly higher elevation than the river. The station throat was marked by an overbridge with a signalbox alongside, beyond which a crossover existed between up and down lines. The down line continued into the platform road, but two sidings radiated off this road near the throat and ran to terminate at the back of the platform. The up road was, of course, used for engine release/run round, and four sidings of differing length radiated from this. One of these served the goods shed. The whole station complex was connected to the main street by an attractive, if later problematical, timber trestle bridge which spanned the Ryburn.

Services and Demise

Little is known about the early trains, but it is recorded that the Jenkins 0-4-2 locomotives worked their last days on the branch, whilst even the GNR-type 0-4-2s were known on goods services. Yet up to 1895 it seems as though the 0-4-4Ts were most in use on the passengers trains. Coaching stock comprised five or six four-wheeled coaches. These were gradually replaced by the Barton Wright 0-6-2Ts with six-wheeled coaches. Barton Wright 0-6-0s also began to take over the goods workings, which were almost entirely the preserve of Sowerby Bridge shed. Things were settling down to a nice steady pattern, but the greatest disappointment was the decision to abandon the scheme for a four-mile long tunnel under Blackstone Edge. So, relegated to a terminal branch line, services became even more localised, and suffered the added disadvantage with advent of tramway services competing with traffic as far as Triangle. Whilst this was not as bad as the Stainland branch, where trams went all the way, motorbus feeder routes began to nibble away at the traffic.

Accordingly the saving grace was again seen in the ubiquitous railmotors (see Chapter 17), which were introduced to the branch service on 1 March 1907. It has been suggested that these services were originally worked by the two Kerr Stuart units, but there is no evidence to support this. By the spring of 1907 the 13 Horwich-built units of George Hughes' design had entered service, and new railmotor services were being introduced as these became available. At this time the Kerr Stuart units were in service in Lancashire, with at least one being at Southport. The confusion may arise from the fact that after the Kerr Stuart units were withdrawn in 1909, the coaches were paired with new Hughes railmotor locomotives. These were then used on the Stainland and Rishworth branches, with the units working back to Low Moor (Bradford) shed at the end of the day. A product of the railmotor service was the aforementioned halt at Watson

Top:
What turned out to be the last passenger train to Rishworth ran on Saturday 5 May 1951 as part of the SLS/MLS 'Pennine Rail Tour'. In addition to trips to Meltham, Stainland and along the Midland branch to Huddersfield, 2-4-2T No 50865 also took the three-coach train of enthusiasts high into the South Pennines. A number of photographs taken on that tour have emerged in recent years, but the author would be delighted to hear from anyone who travelled on that train. *The late Frank Alcock*

Above:
With the road bridge leading to the station already in terminal decay, British Railways were having to face serious questions about the future of the Rishworth branch. With its passenger traffic long withdrawn, the line could only be used for goods traffic and, if the bridge could not carry road vehicles into the terminal goods yard, was the cost of repairs viable. Clearly it was not, so the terminus closed in February 1953, just 21 months after No 50865 is pictured running round the last 'passenger' train. *The late Frank Alcock*

Crossing, along with an immediate increase in the number of services run. On the negative side of the coin, the branch services offered third-class accommodation only. When the railmotors were not available, Aspinall 2-4-2Ts worked the branch with two third-class coaches.

A Halifax-Rishworth bus service introduced in 1926 sounded the death-knell for the passenger trains and, during 1927 and 1928, there were muted suggestions about withdrawal. The matter came to a head in February 1929, following an article in a local paper under the heading 'Ripponden Branch Railway — Should it be closed for passengers?'. The local populace, it seemed, cared little either way; after all in times of economic hardship it was the cheapest services that were of most interest to them. Against this background of apathy the LMS withdrew the service, the last train running on 6 July 1929. Ironically the branch was to have its revenge for, on working back to Halifax empty stock, the train collided with an engine and goods van and managed to block the main line for several hours. This withdrawal signalled the demise of Triangle station and Watson Crossing Halt, but Ripponden and Rishworth stations were converted to goods offices. Considerable levels of parcels traffic continued to and from both stations to a considerable extent and, in the 1930s, two extra motor lorries were transferred to deal with the traffic as part of the railway's country delivery service. Excursion trains continued to operate up the branch, providing a means for local residents to get away on day trips. Later holiday specials were run but not, apparently, after the outbreak of World War 2. Other passenger stock was seen on the branch, but this was only being stored to alleviate pressure on accommodation elsewhere in the district; the up line serving admirably for stabling, particularly in the winter months.

The last passenger trip up to Rishworth is recorded as being the MLS Pennine Rail-Tour of 5 May 1951, when Aspinall 2-4-2T No 50865 visited the terminus. It was almost a 'last rite', for the timber trestle bridge leading to the station was in an atrocious state of repair. Heavy lorries had been banned from crossing it from 1950 onwards, but this did nothing to arrest the decay. Accordingly British Railways, fearing an accident, rightly decided to close the station with effect from 28 February 1952. However, according to *Clinker's Register of Closed Stations*, the date of closure is February 1953. Thereafter trains terminated at Ripponden, where the motor lorry delivery service was then concentrated. These lorries served the outlying districts well and, apart from the removal of the down line in 1954, it seemed as though life would continue as normal. Yet, already freight traffic patterns were changing following the introduction of

A very short afternoon freight slowly pushes its way through the picturesque surroundings behind Sowerby Bridge shed's ex-L&YR 0-6-0 No 52400 on 18 April 1952. To the right of the locomotive will be seen the line's second track, once part of a grand dream for a cut-off route to Rochdale, but now overgrown and weed-strewn. For many years its only use had been to stable coaching stock but, by 1952, even that traffic had long since gone.
Bryan S. Jennings

the Carrier's 'C' Licence in the mid-1950s and the relaxing of speed limits for heavier road freight vehicles, it became increasingly economic to send freight by road. The hidden subsidy of the road building programme being the unfairest form of competition ever faced by the railway. Soon the trains dwindled down to a three or four wagons, mostly of coal, trundling up the branch behind a superannuated ex-L&YR 'A' class 0-6-0 tender engine.

On the excuse of a saving of £2,000 per year, British Railways withdrew the remaining service on 1 September 1958 and the line stood empty and forlorn. Not for long though, as the demolition men moved in and Rishworth station was gone before the 1960s had really commenced. Today little remains of the Rishworth branch, let alone the once grand plan for a main line 'cut off' to Littleborough — like dinosaurs and moral values, it had no place in this brave new world. Even the grandiose station at Sowerby Bridge has largely disappeared as a result of a major fire, whilst passengers on the Halifax-Manchester trains can glimpse the portal of the tunnel adjacent to the station round the side of modern industrial buildings that now occupy the area of the branch platform.

Below:
Where railmotors once stopped, lawnmowers now hover as another pleasant Sunday in the valley settles over the former site of Ripponden station in May 1993. Looking at this view it is hard to imagine that there was a railway here less than three decades ago — but there was. Today, only the retaining wall at the end of the street survives as a clue, though returning on to the street below the abutments of the railway bridge clearly mark its route. *Author*

10 Branches Around Brighouse

In this chapter we will look at three separate branches radiating from the L&YR's Calder Valley main line near Brighouse, each of which were quite individual little lines but had strong thematic links both in constructional and operational terms. The Bradley Wood branch was originally an LNWR line, but the other two were both promoted by the L&YR and came within the later stages of railway development.

Bradley Wood Branch

The construction of this short connecting line — in a reality a spur between the Calder Valley and Huddersfield & Manchester lines — is poorly detailed in local records. It opened in January 1851, having been planned as a means of providing a direct route from Huddersfield to Manchester and thus enabling trains to avoid a reversal at Heaton Lodge. However, by the time the branch opened, the long Standedge Tunnel had been completed and the direct line to Manchester had opened in the summer of 1849. As a result, the LNWR branch was little used at first but, in 1852, a regular goods service was instituted between Huddersfield and Halifax. This continued for a time, with additional workings, such as Huddersfield-Preston freight trains and Huddersfield-Fleetwood excursion services, being operated. Yet, by the end of the decade, the usefulness of the line began to be questioned by the lords and masters at Euston and, in 1859, the branch was consequently closed.

Whilst the route may not have been much value to the LNWR, it was strategically convenient to the L&YR. The Manchester-based company had failed to secure the right to build a line to the town due to its high-handed policies of the 1840s, but it had secured the 13½-mile long Huddersfield & Sheffield Junction Railway route to Penistone. This section of railway was completely isolated from the rest of the L&YR system, and access to it depended on running powers over the LNWR from Heaton Lodge. A major problem in this was the fact that this junction was east-facing and, once again, involved a reversal for trains running to or from Manchester. The Bradley Wood branch would, if it were reopened, resolve all those problems as well

as provide a direct route to Halifax. Yet the real benefits for the company lay in the provision of a direct route to Bradford, the centre of the wool textile trade, which would be free of the encumbrances experienced on the line via Mirfield and the Spen Valley.

In 1860 the L&YR reopened the branch and it was to remain an important artery for through traffic for well over a century. Express, goods and local services all went this way, but it will probably

Below:

With the growing volume of traffic between Huddersfield and Bradford, it became clear at a very early stage that the railway route through the Spen Valley was not going to be adequate. The acquisition of the redundant LNWR branch from Bradley station to Bradley Wood provided the first stage in an alternative, which would be supplemented with the opening of the route from Anchor Pitt to Pickle Bridge in 1881. Even after the Pickle Bridge branch was forced to close, the Bradley Wood branch still saw vital use for freight and some Summer Saturday trains as well as diversionary purposes. In this view a Class 47 with a summer excursion gains the Huddersfield & Manchester line having just come round the branch. *Gavin Morrison*

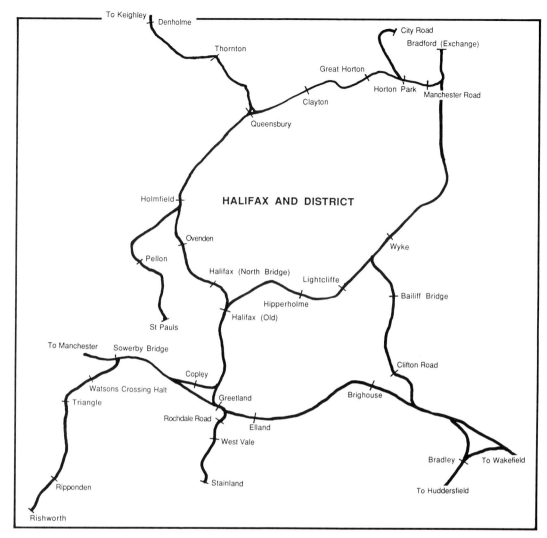

be best known for its rôle as part of the route of the Bradford (Exchange)-London (Marylebone) express services. Along its course ran the famous 'South Yorkshireman' — British Railway's first named train — as well as regular summer-only workings to the south coast resorts. It is perhaps better known locally as being the means of extending services from Penistone, Clayton West, Meltham and Holmfirth beyond Huddersfield to Halifax or Bradford. In conjunction with the Pickle Bridge branch it did this ably for many years, and continued to do so when the powers that be began to doubt the values of a socially-oriented local railway service. Although now officially closed, the track of the branch is still extant today, though we must admit that it is some time since the last of the summer Saturday workings rumbled round its curved course from Bradley Wood Junction to Bradley station. However, it promises to have a

rebirth in store. Though financially frustrated at the present time, there remains a commitment by the West Yorkshire PTE to reintroduce a Halifax-Huddersfield service, with intermediate stations at Elland and Brighouse.

There were no intermediate stations on the line, as it passed through sparsely habited countryside. The branch curved off the main line 1 mile 30 chains southeast of Brighouse station, then passed beneath an overline road bridge carrying a farm track, before progressing on to a level crossing with another farm road. Passing through an attractively wooded area the line curved beneath Lower Quarry Road then dived into the small tunnel which took the railway beneath the A62 Leeds Road. Two more overline bridges were encountered near Bradley Church, before the branch made its junction with the H&M main line immediately east of Bradley station.

Stainland Branch

Chronologically we next encounter the Stainland branch, which was one of the most interesting, if not financially profitable branches, in the whole of the South Pennines. It was conceived as a means of serving one of the textile manufacturing communities which had continued to develop high in the

Top:
After the opening of the Pickle Bridge route between Low Moor and the Calder Valley line, it was hoped that a good level of traffic would develop from its two intermediate stations, Bailiff Bridge and Clifton Road. Yet, strange to relate, much of the expected traffic failed to materialise. Receipts at stations like Clifton Road (for Brighouse) were very badly affected by competition from trams and motor buses and, following a disastrous fire at the station in September 1931, it was closed completely. *B. C. Lane Collection*

Above:
The other station on the line, at Bailiff Bridge, pictured here in the earlier years of the century, fared even worse. It was a casualty of the wartime closures to reduce staffing requirements during 1917. When one looks at the assemblage of staff awaiting the arrival of the train in this picture it is not difficult to imagine how the manpower savings could be achieved. *B. C. Lane Collection.*

Pennines at a time when most of the others had migrated down into the valleys. Nearer the wool crop it may have been, but it was an awfully long way from a readily available supply of cheap coal. Local coal mines at first staved off the need for migration, but these were soon worked out and a railway was seen as the only means of salvation. To this end an Act of Parliament was obtained on 5 July 1865 — the same act also included the Rishworth branch. However, the L&YR's pecuniary financial position and a depressed local market did little to stimulate development at that time. At a meeting of the L&YR's directors and shareholders on 25 May 1870, Mr G. Wilson (chairman) told the audience that they proposed to raise £140,000 for the Stainland and Ripponden branches and that land had already been purchased to this end.

Work was not as arduous as it might have been thought and, following the passage of the second Act of Parliament on 16 July 1874, work progressed quickly. The two major works of construction were two viaducts of 179yd and 230yd in length, but surprisingly the branch was extravagantly laid out as double track throughout. The 1¾-mile long branch from Greetland to Stainland opened on 1 January 1875 and at once attracted considerable levels of freight traffic coal and woollen yarn inwards, textiles (mostly worsted cloth) and stone outwards. Sadly passenger traffic never really caught on in any great way, the countryside was too sparse for that, even though six trains a day were provided at the outset. Most of the local populace worked in the woollen mills, and those who travelled to work usually did so on foot. Shopping excursions to West Vale or Halifax were almost unheard of at any time other than Saturday afternoon. Mingled in with this were the men folk, who in the season, would catch the train to go off and support their local football team. In this case it would be either Halifax Town or Huddersfield Town, local loyalties being equally and fiercely divided. However, since both sets of supporters wore blue and white knitted scarves it was hard to tell who followed who.

The difficulties with the branch passenger service were symptomatic of the railway's decline in this regard, as it was never really designed to cater for the traffic. Freight was its main reason for being, and the L&YR made little pretence otherwise. However, when competition from Halifax's municipal trams began to erode the already poor levels of local passenger support, the company actually became quite concerned. Accordingly it was decided to convert the branch passenger service to railmotor operation as early as 1 March 1907, with a new halt being opened at Rochdale Road to supplement the main stations at West Vale and Stainland & Holywell Green. Actually this

Above:

Working through to Stainland, Hughes railmotor No 4 stands in Halifax station c1910. The atmospheric view captures the era well, with the station gas lamps and notice boards all proclaiming this to be Halifax. The destination board on the trailer coach tells passengers that this is the Halifax & Stainland service, whilst there would be plenty of staff about to give directions if needed. All of which is quite a contrast with the poor facility which masquerades as Halifax station today. Worthy of note are the retractable steps on the side of the trailer which would give a means of access at the rail-level halts provided on the branch.
B. C. Lane Collection

Above left:

The junction of the Halifax and Stainland branches was found at Greetland, which was once quite an important station on the Calder Valley main line. It was always a good place to watch the trains go by, either as a train-spotter or a photographer. In July 1951 one of Accrington's 'Black 5' 4-6-0s No 45367 heads over the junction on a Wakefield-Burnley stopping train. *The late Frank Alcock*

Left:

The first stopping place   on the Stainland branch was the well-laid out station at West Vale. Never overly busy after the introduction of electric tram services, the station struggled on in competition with the tram and bus stops in the town centre. Pictured not long before the LMS withdrew the service in September 1929, Hughes railmotor No 10614 simmers at West Vale with its two-coach train. Remarkably, the goods services at the station lasted quite a while longer, being withdrawn three decades later on 14 September 1959.
Author's Collection

Above:
Another view of No 10614, but this time working with just its single trailer coach as it stands at Stainland in the late 1920s. Once again note the substantial warehouse and the stone-construction of the station buildings, all structures that were built to last. The child's push-chair pictured in the view also looks to be quite a substantial construction and much more sturdy than today's creations. *B. C. Lane Collection*

Above:
In L&YR days railmotor No 3 is seen at the Stainland terminus, its attractive design clearly evident. Of some interest is the original condition of the trailer coach with its fully glazed end. This feature did not appear on the later trailer cars, as an end connection was provided so that a second trailer car could be added if needed. The full front must have offered the driver excellent panoramic views on scenic lines such as those to Stainland and Rishworth. *B. C. Lane Collection*

was, by a matter of minutes, the first L&YR branch in Yorkshire to convert to the Hughes-designed railmotors (Rishworth came next), and was only the sixth on the whole railway system. The railmotors revived local fortunes for a while, but tram competition continued to erode away the basic services and passengers dwindled. At the Grouping some 16 trains left the terminus for Halifax, with one short-ened working running just as far as the junction station at Greetland. However, the stringent years of the post-Grouping era soon had the LMS evaluating the passenger service, and, after two reprieves, it was finally withdrawn on 23 September 1929.

That was not the end of the branch, nor indeed passenger traffic over it. For many years the local Cooperative Society combined with local schools and the band to run special excursion trains to resorts as diverse as Llandudno, Blackpool, Windermere, Bangor, Coniston and Belle Vue Zoo. My wife's grandparents, residents of the area, were among those who enjoyed such excursions, but recall their connection as being with the 'Sunday School Treat'. Freight traffic remained consistently based on coal going up the valley, and parcels of cloth, wrapped in thick brown paper tied up with stout pieces of string, being sent outwards. Unfortunately, the vehicles used for this traffic were not compatible with each other and there was, as a result, a lot of empty stock working on the line. One line of the double track was all that was needed for the pick-up goods working, so the other was utilised for the storage of spare or condemned stock; much of which was waiting to be sent to the carriage and wagon works at Thornhill, near Dewsbury. However, as traffic trends changed the trains

dwindled to just a couple of wagons at a time. Eventually the branch completely closed on 14 September 1959, outliving its near neighbour the Rishworth branch by a year. A fanciful scheme to use the branch in connection with the massive M62 and Scammonden Dam construction programmes in the 1960s was never likely to become reality, so the trackbed was left alone — slowly being reclaimed by the Pennine countryside from which it was hewn.

The Clifton Road or Pickle Bridge Branch
Officially known as the Clifton Road branch, this line, which left the Calder Valley line 1 mile 26 chains east of Brighouse station, will always be remembered as the Pickle Bridge branch. Its position between the Halifax-Low Moor line at Wyke and the main line made it an immediate success. Yet, its construction also led to its downfall, due entirely to the needles intransigence of just one landowner. First envisaged as part of the West Riding Union Railways of 1846, the line was to be several years in the development. The failure of the WRU to make satisfactory progress down the valley from Wyke led to another proposal in the 1860s, which culminated in an L&YR Act of 1866 for a branch from the main line up to a point on the north side of Brighouse. This terminus would have been where Clifton Road was eventually built but, thankfully, this truncated scheme also failed. This left the way open for a full 'cut-off' route in order to provide a direct Huddersfield-Bradford service, and this was finally achieved on 21 July 1873 when the 3¾-mile long branch was authorised. However, here comes our uncooperative landowner, who

meddled with the Act to such an extent that a further piece of legislation was required in 1875. It resulted in the junction being built on the Halifax side of the valley, which in turn demanded a totally unnecessary viaduct to get back to Bailiff Bridge. This was not a little viaduct either, for a massive 22-arch structure was required.

Difficulties were evident in the construction of the viaduct, and these continued down to its early demise. However, the line duly opened on 1 March 1881 with intermediate stations at Clifton Road (for Brighouse) and Bailiff Bridge. At the junction with the Halifax line the station of Pickle Bridge bestowed upon the branch its unusual name which stuck until the closure, even though the station changed its guise to Wyke in 1882. Despite the ruling gradient of 1 in 70 most of the local passenger workings mentioned earlier, were routed over it. However, its most important trains were the L&YR/GCR express services to Marylebone, and the through workings to the southern coast that included GWR and LBSCR coaching stock. Bailiff Bridge lost its passenger service as a wartime economy measure in 1917, and they were never reinstated. A catastrophic fire resulted in the destruction of Clifton Road Station on 14 September 1931 and, in view of the poor economic climate, a decision was taken to close it rather than rebuild it. Whilst this effectively meant that the branch had lost its passenger service, the local stopping trains passing over it to destinations between Bradford and Sheffield actually increased. In addition the line was still heavily used as a through route for both express passenger trains and goods.

Unfortunately, after Nationalisation in 1948 the problems of Wyke Viaduct re-emerged with potentially catastrophic results. The poor condition of the structure was causing dire concern to the Chief Civil Engineer's Department at Bradford, as further subsidence of the piers was becoming evident. Four of the 22 arches were already 'out of true', whilst two were showing signs of bad cracks. As a result, the remaining passenger services were rerouted via Halifax or the Spen Valley line and, without any further delay or plans for reinstatement, the viaduct was closed completely on 4 August 1952. Despite the condition of the bridge being the ostensible reason for the line's closure, the structure was to survive for more than 30 years with a distinct 'Gothic Arch' indicating the structural problems. Ironically, though the 'damaged' section was subsequently demolished, half of the viaduct was left standing like some 18th century folly. Today its remains leave an ugly scar across the landscape and we might well ask, where else could something so ludicrous happen but Britain?

Whilst the line had been out of use for more than 20 years, during the early 1970s, with the east-

ward construction of the M62 through the area resulting in the temporary severing of the Spen Valley line between Low Moor and Cleckheaton, serious consideration was given to the reopening of the Pickle Bridge branch in order to save the cost of a new bridge over the motorway. In the event the latter was built, although, ironically, it was to see only relatively little use as freight traffic from Bradford plummeted in the late 1970s.

Below:
The last passenger train up the Stainland Branch was, like the Rishworth line, worked by No 50865 on the SLS/MLS 'Pennine Rail Tour'. Few views of it working up towards Stainland seem to have surfaced, so this view of the train standing at the terminus is particularly pleasing. Once again the engine sports its LMS livery, despite the fact that nearly three and a half years have elapsed since Nationalisation. *The late Frank Alcock*

Bottom:
Holywell Green Viaduct pictured in May 1993, a redundant asset in the days of the motorcar, lorry and bus. By poignant contrast, the narrow metalled road from which the view was taken is no longer available to vehicular traffic — it has crumbled away and fallen into the fields below. *Author*

11 The Holcombe Brook Branch

Conception and Construction

The branch to Holcombe Brook has to be one of the most remarkable pieces of railway described in this book, for its history is quite without parallel. To the northwest of Bury lies the dividing point between the West Pennines and the South Pennines, and here are to be found two tributary streams of the River Irwell. The southern stream, Kirklees Brook, joins the Irwell near Bury, having flowed east through the villages of Greenmount, Tottington and Woolfold. The northern watercourse Holcombe Brook passes through a village that bears the same name as the stream, then runs down to join the Irwell near Summerseat.

A glance at the map of the locality might indicate that the development of a railway to Holcombe Brook would have logically assumed a junction at Summerseat, with a short branch of a mile or so in length to reach the small town. However, the first promotion was in fact for a Bury & Tottington District Railway, which only offered an extension to Holcombe Brook as a secondary objective to its overall purpose. The BT&DR Act was Authorised on 2 August 1877, with power to build three railways: Railway No 1, which was 3 miles 3 furlongs long, was to run from the L&YR line at Bury to Holcombe Brook; No 2 would be just over a mile long and run from Woolfold past Olive Brothers Wagon Works; however, Railway No 3 remains something of a mystery, the papers for this part of the Act being missing. Perhaps this is irrelevant anyway, for the main landowner in the area, the Earl of Derby, petitioned against railways Nos 2 and 3, and was instrumental in having their powers revoked. Accordingly, only the line to Holcombe Brook was to be built, with the first sod of the project being cut on 26 July 1878.

It was only now that the troubles really began, for within 15 months the contractor building the line suddenly went out of business, though details about his demise are scant. The work was then awarded to J. M. Smith in November 1880. This was an action the BT&DR would later regret. Smith certainly had his work cut out, for the three-

Left:

Buckley Wells, Bury, was the former engineering base of the East Lancashire Railway. The original locomotive works, alongside the line leading to Bury Bolton Street station, were converted to an electric car running depot in 1915-16, in preparation for the conversion of the line to a third-rail service from Manchester to Bury. Alongside stood a steam locomotive depot which originated from 1876 but, by 1960, it had become home to DMUs as well as steam engines. Prior to its closure the shed was used to store several historic locomotives, such as Nos 45596 *Bahamas*, E27000 *Electra*, E27005 *Minerva* and E26000 *Tommy*, which is pictured here on 2 April 1972.
Gordon Coultas

Above:

The first conversion of the Holcombe Brook branch, to an overhead electric system, took place on an experimental basis in July 1913. The equipment was all provided by Dick Kerr, but the stock into which the traction motors were fitted was built by the L&YR at Newton Heath to Diagrams 133 (motor coaches) and 134 (trailer coaches). The motor coaches were numbered 3500/1 and the trailers 3600/1 and seated 75 and 85 passengers respectively. Only the motor coaches had pantographs, as this view of No 3501 taken at Brandlesholme Road Halt shows.
B. C. Lane Collection

Below:

After the experiments with the Dick Kerr system, the L&YR considered the branch had the potential to generate more traffic if it were converted to the Manchester-Bury third-rail system. This was completed by 29 March 1918, but there was no additional stock built especially for the Holcombe Brook service. Two-car and three-car sets worked the branch and, sometimes, the services were comprised of five or six-car formations. The electric service on the Holcombe Brook branch was withdrawn in July 1951, and passenger services completely finished on 4 May 1952. On that date one of the branch line's former workhorses — M29210 — stands at Bury Bolton Street.
Gordon Coultas

mile long line was an exceptionally difficult one to build. In addition to the Woolfold Viaduct, there were also major difficulties with two large embankments at Leemans Hill and Sunny Wood. Smith was under pressure both from the terrain and the directors of the BT&DR, and a certain Mr Wallis who seized the rails and property of the company by an order of the Sheriff. Finances of both contractor and railway were in a perilous state, a matter which can not have been helped by the fact that only £37,000 of the BT&DR's envisaged £57,000 of stock had been subscribed. Fortunately the company were allowed powers to raise an extra £53,000 by a combination of shares and mortgages. This acquired, the work progressed to its completion with Tottington Viaduct being the last major piece of work to be finished.

Inspection by Maj Mandarin of the Board of Trade sanctioned the opening of the line for early October 1882. The directors of the company now saw a chance of getting some revenue from the line, but they had not reckoned with the dissatisfaction of their contractor Smith. On 2 October he objected to the opening of the line, claiming he had not been fully paid for his work — the company retorted he had been overpaid. Eventually, Smith was persuaded to withdraw his objection, on the basis that he would be given a Lloyds Bond of second preference shares *in lieu* of the cash owed. Accordingly the line was opened on 6 November, but the cash-strapped railway company did so without any expenditure on 'unnecessary celebrations'. However, two special excursions were run to Belle Vue in Manchester by local companies.

Smith was still an unhappy man and, on 29 December, he issued an ultimatum that he had to be paid forthwith or he would stop maintaining the line as per his contract. The L&YR, who were running trains for the BT&DR, quickly pointed out that unless the line was maintained they would have to withdraw the service. However, it appeared as though they would be happy to do this work, on the proviso that all expenses were met out of the BT&DR's share of the revenue. The BT&DR had no choice but to agree. Smith filed a writ for £30,000 against the company in the High Court on 17 February 1883, and this was followed by further claims from the Consolidated Bank and the Bury Saw Mills, though the railway's other main creditors, the L&YR, did not join in the action. The railway then had to raise a further £60,000 to pay off its debts, of which £38,000 was issued to Smith in the form of third-class stock. Reliance on the L&YR had now become extremely heavy, so it was not surprising that the line was absorbed by the Manchester company; it is perhaps less understandable that the railway maintained its independence until July 1888.

The Line Described

The branch left the L&YR main line by a double junction 726yd north of Bury's Bolton Street station, beyond which an area of sidings existed on both sides of the line. One of the sidings on the north side was 'lengthened' towards the end of the last century in order to provide a private delivery facility to a factory at Fernhill which had been transformed from an iron foundry into a chemical works. Meanwhile on the southern side, one siding was 'looped' to serve the Peel Mills. Beyond these sidings the line crossed the Irwell by a five-arch viaduct, and whilst this only had a single-track deck, it is of interest to note that the piers were built in such a way as to accommodate a two-line crossing at some later stage. The line then began to climb on a ruling 1 in 50 gradient before coming to a point where a wrought-iron over-line road bridge crossed the railway. At this point Woodhill Halt would be opened in 1905. This station was opera-

Above:
With the end of its passenger service in sight, Woolfold station is pictured just before closure. The passing loop has obviously seen little traffic in recent times and the former down platform is evidently long out of use, although the third rail is still in place on the main running line. After the final train, on 4 May, the only passenger train to venture this way would be an RCTS special on 26 July 1953. *Gordon Coultas*

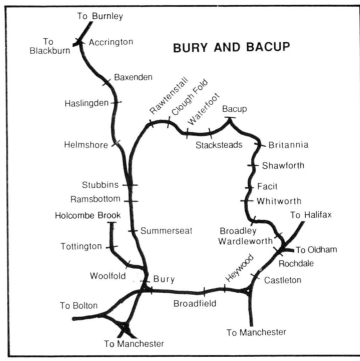

tional until 1 April 1918. Despite its early closure, a new platform was erected on the opposite side of the bridge in 1934 to serve workers from a nearby mill.

Heading due west now, the line crossed a tributary of the local canal by another wrought-iron bridge, before entering a rock cutting crossed by an over-line bridge carrying Brandlesholme Road. On the opposite side of the bridge lay Brandlesholme Road Halt, also opened in 1905, with a rail-level platform. Like Woodhill Halt this was replaced, in the mid-1930s, by another wooden sided platform with cinder top and basic shelter. Beyond the halt the railway was built to single-track formation as it curved northwestwards to Woolfold station, crossing a five-arch stone viaduct *en route*. The largest station on the line, Woolfold, was considered to be roughly the half-way stage, so a two-platform layout was provided to facilitate the passing of branch trains. The goods yard was located on the down side of the station, with its throat facing Holcombe Brook. One long siding ran parallel with the branch line, and towards its southern end this had a loop, one leg of which passed through the goods shed. Three other sidings were provided, all of which curved away from station throat at about 75°. The main station buildings, situated on the down platform, were largely made of wood, but the end walls were of local brick.

From Woolfold the line continued northwest passing through farming land to the delightfully named Sunny Wood Halt, which was also opened to coincide with the introduction of railmotor services. After this the line climbed steadily for a short distance, eventually levelling off before it pulled into the station at Tottington. The goods layout here was similar to that at Woolfold, except that its throat faced towards Bury, and it had two dead-end sidings instead of three. The goods shed had a similar loop arrangement, but this was removed around 1908-9, when the shed siding became a dead-end road. The passengers were catered for by a 280ft long curved platform, again furnished with predominantly wooden-built buildings. An over-line road bridge at the Holcombe Brook end of the platform carried Kirklees Street above the railway, which then curved away in a shallow cutting towards Robert's Siding.

From the siding, which served the Stormer Hill Bleach Works of R. K. Roberts Ltd, the line passed on to Tottington Viaduct, a structure of nine arches spanning a reservoir. Like the first viaduct on the branch, this structure also had piers built to accommodate a double-track deck, though only a single one was ever built. On the far side the line curved round past the entry to Knowles Siding and a nearby level crossing, before it eventually progressed to Greenmount. Smallest of the original sta-

Top:
Greenmount station, with the 9.38am train arriving from Holcombe Brook, pictured in the early 1900s. The locomotive is a Barton Wright 0-4-4T from Bury shed, hauling a train of six-wheeled stock. The station building is of a typically frugal design, with brick built ends and a timber face. There is no station canopy, but the building has an attractive valance which would be picked out in the umber/tan colour scheme adopted by the L&YR. *B. C. Lane Collection*

Above:
In its last month of operations the branch was largely worked by Aspinall 2-4-2Ts which ran with a two-coach train of compartment stock. Just a few days from the end No 50651 propels a Holcombe Brook motor train away from Woolfold. *J. Davenport*

tions on the line, Greenmount had a single siding for goods traffic, and a slightly curved passenger platform. An over-line bridge at the Holcombe Brook end was, like many others on the line, built to permit a double line of rails to pass below it. A climb of 1 in 40 then took the line up to Holcombe Brook, where a single platform terminus existed. The main buildings were up a ramp from the plat-

Above:

The terminus at Holcombe Brook was, in many ways, quite a spartan one. Its goods yard, pictured above the train shown here, was tiny compared to facilities provided at similar sized villages like Meltham (Chapter 5). The limited nature of the yard is clearly seen in this April 1952 view, with the coal drops, timber-built goods warehouse (complete with a serious list) and weigh-house all visible.
J. Davenport

Above:

With little future left in store, the branch would serve only goods traffic after May 1952, and even that would soon be eroded away. So this study of motor-fitted 2-4-2T No 50655 illustrates well the branch in its dying days. What a pity it could not have managed to last until the introduction of DMUs; if it had the story might have been quite different. *J. Davenport*

form and set at a 90° angle to the railway, this often gives the impression (in some photographs), that the terminus was devoid of station buildings. The goods yard once again followed a similar pattern to its two contemporaries on the branch but, like Tottington, it also only had two dead-end sidings. Yet, because of the steep gradient leading back down to Greenmount, the head shunt of the yard was built at a much higher elevation than the running lines, so as to prevent runaways.

Services and Demise

The line was worked from the outset by the L&YR, though it would appear that many of the early locomotives were of East Lancashire Railway origin. This is probable as the latter company had been absorbed into the L&YR in 1859. It will be appreciated that these were therefore of some antiquity, so the newer Barton Wright 0-4-4Ts and 0-6-2Ts soon made an appearance. Four-wheel coaches quickly gave way to six-wheel stock. The maximum number of six-wheel coaches over the line was 10. Aspinall 2-4-2Ts were introduced around the turn of the century, though photographic evidence seems to infer that the 0-4-4Ts from Bury shed provided the mainstay for motive power on passenger trains at least. Competition from tram services between Bury and Tottington provided a constant threat to the railway's passenger traffic. This competition was countered in 1905 by the introduction of a railmotor service. The three aforementioned halts were opened that year, as were two others at Footpath Crossing and Knowles Crossing. This allowed the maintenance of an extensive service

between Bury and Holcombe Brook, which amounted to no less than 22 trains per day.

In 1912 the Preston-based company of Dick Kerr, perhaps better known for tramcar manufacture, approached the L&YR to ask for facilities to experiment with electric rail traction on a steeply graded line. This company had recently won a contract for Brazil, so they needed facilities to test and evaluate an overhead system. A sub-station was erected at Holcombe Brook, where power was converted to 3,500/3,600V dc and fed to the overhead wire through a Dick Kerr 525kW generator. Stock for the Holcombe Brook project was built at the L&YR's Newton Heath Carriage Works, with two two-car sets being produced. These comprised a motor coach and a trailer coach, each 60ft long, the motor-car having two pantographs. The Dick Kerr system commenced operations in July 1913 and was eventually sold to the L&YR for a sum of c£6,000 in 1916. By this time the L&YR had already decided to introduce a third-rail electric traction system between Manchester Victoria and Bury. Accordingly it was intended to convert that branch to the same system but before conversion could take place a novel traction arrangement was introduced as a temporary measure, as a result of the failure of the Holcombe Brook sub-station. At Bury a wire was fed from the 1,200V dc third-rail system to the overhead wires of the Holcombe Brook branch. A Bury line power car was then coupled with a Dick Kerr motor-coach, though the latter was used only as a trailer car which picked up the power for the Bury unit through its pantographs.

The conversion was completed by 1918 with the third-rail service commencing on 29 March This did not, however, signal the demise of the Dick Kerr sets. These were put into store at Bury and were later rebuilt by the LMS as experimental diesel-electric sets. In 1928 they were put on trial services between Blackpool and Lytham but, sadly, they met with little success and were only used spasmodically until their withdrawal the following Easter. The replacement service of Bury electric cars was still as intensive as ever, but the rail-level halts along the line were now of no practical use as the new stock did not have the retractable steps of either the railmotors or the Dick Kerr sets. Accordingly platforms had to be provided at Brandlesholme Road and Sunny Wood, but the others were closed on 1 April 1918. The usual formation for the branch was a two-car set, though sometimes three-car sets were employed. At busy times when visitors from Manchester came up to walk on the nearby moors the trains could be made up from eight vehicles, formed by two three-car sets and one two-car set. The line and its electric sets continued to serve the area well for the next 33 years, but one day early in 1951 it was suddenly announced that the electric units were to be suspended for 'equipment renewals'. The suspension came in March and the units were never reintroduced. Steam was brought back in to fill the gap, though it should be said that it had never been taken off the goods services as the various yards and sidings were never electrified.

The line had been feeling the pinch since Bury Corporation replaced the Tottington trams with motor buses in 1948. This conversion resulted in 20,000 passengers a year deserting the railways in favour of the new bus service. After the demise of the electric units, the branch passenger service reverted to the 2-4-2Ts, which were often accompanied by converted trailers from the Hughes railmotors. Atrociously timed connections at Bury saw the Manchester trains pulling out of the platform moments before the Holcombe Brook trains arrived, whilst journey times on the branch were increased by up to 50%. Despite plans for massive housing development all along the branch line's corridor, the service was withdrawn on 26 July 1953. Goods trains continued to trundle up the gradient to Holcombe Brook until 2 May 1960, when the line was truncated to terminate at Tottington. It all came to an end on 17 August 1963 when the branch was closed completely, its track was ripped up and yet another national asset was squandered. One can only speculate on how much people travelling on the congested roads through the area today, would have welcomed the opportunity of an extended Metrolink service out to Tottington and Holcombe Brook.

Below:
On the last train a youthful fireman looks back down the platform from the cab of No 50651. The cobbled platform and the booking hall at the top of the ramp are soon to be redundant, as more of our national transport network slipped silently into oblivion. *Gordon Coultas*

Bottom:
Not that you'd guess it, but this was once the station site. Its role today is far different from that which was envisaged by the promoters of the Tottington & District Railway. What future would the line have had if its formation had been retained and left undeveloped. Might it have seen the extension of the Manchester Light Railway system Metrolink? Surely this proves the case that local planning authorities should refuse any application that might interfere with the trackbed of old railways or canals which future generations may consider an invaluable asset. *Paul D. Shannon*

12 The Bacup Branches

Conception and Construction

The town of Bacup lays roughly eight miles north-east of Bury as the crow flies, whilst the same bird would take about seven miles to make the journey from Rochdale heading a northwesterly direction. As railways were promoted to both these towns, it became logical for further developments to encompass the traffic-rich districts of the upper Rossendale Valley. Bacup, with extensive textile and stone quarrying industries, was seen as a rich target for freight traffic. It was just a matter of who got there first. The contender in the Bury corner was the East Lancashire Railway, whilst in Rochdale it was their old rivals the L&YR. The former had the potentially easier route but, even so, the course the railway was to take would involve substantial civil engineering. The L&YR route up through Whitworth was what you would call difficult to say the least — one imagines that the navvies who toiled their way up the valley called it much worse.

The ELR also had a head start, for they had reached Rawtenstall in September 1846 — five miles more would take them to their goal. The necessary Act of Parliament for this line was passed in July 1846, while the Manchester & Leeds Railway (forerunner of the L&YR) also got its Act for a line from Rochdale. Neither of them began work at once, although the ELR did commence their branch the following year though it was only a single line of rails built on a double-track formation. By May financial problems were besetting the project, so the work beyond Newchurch was suspended. The M&L meanwhile were becoming worried about a proposed alternate route into Rochdale, so it ignored its Bacup proposals to counter the threat. The ELR went on and opened a track to Newchurch in March 1848, but Bacup still provided an alluring target. Despite the necessity for three lengthy tunnels (with the trio having a combined total length of over a quarter of mile), work began in September 1851 and the single line opened to Bacup the following October. By now the M&L had become the L&YR, who viewed the ELR's encroachment into an area it had 'set its cap at' with sanguinary intent!

However, by 1859 the ELR and L&YR had amalgamated and, at last, when it seemed as there would be no need for a route from Rochdale, the

Left:
The next series of pictures takes a semi-circular tour from Rochdale to Bury along the two Bacup branches. The first view is taken just near Wardleworth, north of Rochdale, with Ivatt 2-6-0 No 46437 and brake van making a light train on the newly ballasted track just beyond the station.
Richard S. Greenwood

L&YR decided to pick up its original scheme and submitted the proposals to Parliament. Royal Assent for a branch was granted on 30 June 1862, but this was only allowed to Shawforth and, in the event, it would only be taken to Facit. Work on the scheme did not proceed quickly, the rugged terrain threw enough spanners into the works to ensure that. One such 'spanner' was the Roch Viaduct where problems with the piers provided continual frustrations. Yet, by the autumn of 1870, the railway had opened to Facit and, inside two years of this event, Parliament approved the rest of the line up to Bacup. Approval was one thing, building was another. Difficult as the terrain was going to be, acquiring the land on which to build the railway in the first place was to be even more problematical. Landowners now had a fairly high expectancy for the price of land sold for railway development, the asking prices were exorbitant — though in the end arbitration courts reduced the claims by up to half. As a consequence contracts could not be let until May 1878, by which time the ex-ELR line to Bacup was being doubled. One of the difficulties in this was the construction of the 592yd-long Thrutch Tunnel, needed to duplicate the full length of the two shorter bores at Newchurch.

In view of the doubling of the Stubbins-Bacup section and the imminent arrival of the branch from Rochdale, Bacup station was completely rebuilt in 1881. The Board of Trade inspected the Rochdale line in October, but the inspector did not like the timber trestle near Bacup and ordered it be filled in as soon as possible. With that proviso the Bacup-Rochdale service commenced on 1 December 1881 — a mere 35 years after it had been first approved! Like many new lines, the railway stimulated indus-

Above:
This late 1960s view perhaps typifies the extent to which many of the Pennine branch lines had decayed, as the road revolution sealed the fate of many secondary rail routes. As an unidentified '08' shunter draws a rake of empty 16-ton steel mineral wagons beneath Wardleworth signalbox, the devastation is all too evident. The magnificent elevated box has become the object of attention for missile throwing youths, and even the 'netty' door has succumbed. This was a disposable age, in heritage terms at least, and so much of value was wastefully squandered — what wouldn't some preserved railway give for a structure like this today! *Richard S. Greenwood*

Right:
Our next study, taken at Tong Lane Crossing between Whitworth and Facit, again tells a story of the mid-1960s in northern England. Time-honoured '4F' No 43903 might have been, but then it was just another feature of a dirty industrial landscape. Even the level crossing gates, often depicted in gleaming brilliant white paint on many scale models, bear the filth and scars of a generation of industry. Yet this scene is powerful in both emotion and nostalgia, for this is the way it really was.
Richard S. Greenwood

Right:

A small shed was opened by the East Lancashire Railway at Bacup but, when the line through to Rochdale opened in 1882, it had to be replaced by a more suitable facility. This was erected on the Rochdale branch close to the mouth of the tunnel leading to Britannia. The six-road shed had a long association with the Aspinall 2-4-2Ts, such as No 50829 pictured at the 'coal hole' on 2 October 1954. The shed had, at this time, less than a week to live and, by now, its allocation was down to eight engines — four LMS 2-6-4Ts, two ex-L&YR 0-6-0s and two 2-4-2Ts (Nos 50647/50829). *J. Davenport*

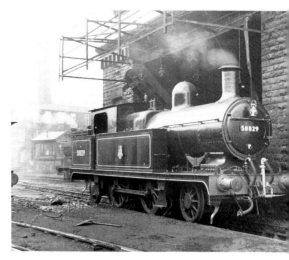

Centre right:

With the withdrawal of the Bacup passenger services officially to take place two days later, the branch was to go out with a bang and not a whimper. To celebrate its passing a rail tour special, hauled by Ivatt Class 2MT 2-6-0 No 46437 and Stanier Class 4MT 2-6-4T No 42644, visited the branch. *J. Davenport*

Bottom right:

Where was there a station, then? This might be an appropriate question to ask when looking at this view. Taken from the brow of a hill above the River Irwell, it shows the site of the old station with what was the platform area now covered by the long, low modern building in the centre of the picture. Another dramatic comparison with the past is the absence of mill chimneys that tower above Bacup; in this 1986 view only one still stands, a quarter of a century earlier around 10 would have been visible from the same vantage point. *Paul D. Shannon*

trial development to such an extent that the manufacturing capacity of the district grew 287% between 1871 and 1881. The additional traffic outstripped all the existing facilities, and within a few months of the Rochdale line opening a new engine shed had to be provided between the station and Britannia.

The Lines Described

To describe the lines in detail would not be possible in the short space available, but an imaginary journey from Ramsbottom to Rochdale should present a flavour of the two fascinating branches. Leaving Ramsbottom the Bacup train rumbled up through Stubbins Junction, where the ELR line to Accrington and the north diverged. For a good while the two lines ran parallel with each other, though at different levels, before crossing the River Irwell. Some little distance further on the Accrington line recrossed the river and curved away to Helmshore, but the Bacup line stayed on its eastern bank and passed Irwell Vale sidings. The line then continued on to Ewood Bridge & Edenfield station, twice crossing the Irwell where the river looped just before the station. A small goods yard here was originally provided with a stone-built warehouse, though this was inconveniently situated and it was replaced in the late 19th century with an inferior timber structure. As the line progressed towards Rawtenstall, two private delivery sidings were passed at Horncliffe and Townsend Fold, both of which were primarily concerned with stone traffic from nearby quarries.

Another crossing of the Irwell took the line into Rawtenstall, the present day terminus of the preserved East Lancashire Railway. This station originally had just a single platform, but with the doubling of the branch it was considerably extended. Goods facilities were likewise improved to meet the growing traffic levels, whilst, beyond the station, a number of substantial private sidings were established. The signalbox for one of these, Ilex Hall Carr Cabin, was actually erected on piles sunk in the bed of the River Irwell.

Yet another crossing of the river took the line to the island platform of Clough Fold, behind which stood a small goods yard. The line then had to pass over the Irwell three more times until it came to Waterfoot Goods Yard, where a substantial three-storey warehouse was provided. The original goods yard for Waterfoot (Newchurch) had been adjacent to the station but, when the line was doubled, the land on which it stood was needed for the expansion. Accordingly the station which stood beyond yet another crossing of the Irwell, retained only three sidings to serve local coal traffic. The station stood in an elevated position between river and the main street and, to my mind, presents one of the most fascinating prototypes for those interested in authentic railway modelling. Beyond the station yet another crossing of the Irwell led directly into the Newchurch/Thrutch tunnel complex. On emerging from the hill, the line ran on to Stacksteads station. At Stacksteads the island platform was actually built across the Irwell. The station had sidings at either end, from where inclined tramways led up the hillsides to stone quarries.

Now running on the north side of the river, the line pressed on to make a double crossing of yet another loop in the Irwell, beyond which it reached Holt's Siding (stone traffic). It then made its 15th and penultimate crossing of the Irwell before diving into Bacup Tunnel. It had been intended to build a second bore here when the line was doubled but, in the end, the original tunnel was widened. On the opposite side the branch curved round past the goods yard, where a substantial goods shed stood until January 1959 when it was destroyed by a fire. Beyond the goods yard the line was joined by the Rochdale branch, and then it had one last entanglement with the Irwell before finally pulling into Bacup station. This was never really what might be called a grand terminus, just a two-sided platform

Above:

On the road down to Bury came Clough Fold, an attractive little station which always generated a good return for the railway if, for no other reason, than its location was alongside the main street and, thereby, just as convenient as the tram stops. The L&YR had found the answer to competing with the trams by means of its railmotor trains and, even when these had been withdrawn, the concept was continued by motor-fitted 2-4-2Ts and 2-6-2Ts. Such a scene is captured on 14 April 1955 with No 58029 on a Bury-Bacup working. Yet, it was the DMUs which brought life, and patronage, back to the branch. Ironically, despite their popularity and level of use, Beeching saw no place for a Bacup service and earmarked it for closure. *C. J. Allen*

with an overall canopy — for good measure the cattle pens were located directly opposite. But even so it was much better than the 'miserable hovel' that had stood here between 1852 and 1881.

Crossing the platform at Bacup we find the Rochdale train waiting, its journey holding out the promise of more rugged scenery, with a mixture of cotton mills and stone quarries. A slam of the door, the shrill blast of a whistle and the train eases out of the station, curving left over the point work alongside India Mill. A sharp curve takes the line round past Ross's cotton mills on the left, which had a long curved siding sneaking round from the engine shed to carry in coal and bales of raw cotton. The engine shed comes next, also to the left, where the four roads once held as many as 40 engines. It had an allocation of 37 engines at the Grouping, but the demise of the Rochdale passenger service drove the final nails into its coffin and closure came in 1954. Rumbling through the tunnel the train emerges into Britannia station. Britannia had an island platform, which closed as a wartime 'economy' measure in 1917 and never reopened. A stone siding from nearby quarries fared somewhat better; having opened in 1884 it lasted until towards the end of World War 2.

South of Britannia the summit of the line was reached at 967ft, which incidentally was also the highest point on the L&YR. The descent down to Shawforth took the twin-track railway into a station, where stone traffic was again a constant feature. Next came Facit, once the terminus of the line, and where substantial stone traffic was generated. The sidings established to serve this traffic were quite extensive for such a little station, whilst a rope-operated self-acting incline provided a connection with the quarry lines on the moors above. In itself the local sandstone traffic and the private railways laid in to serve the quarries, could occupy a full book in their own right — but we must suffice with the understanding that it was this traffic alone that gave substance and impetus to the L&YR's decision to build the Rochdale-Bacup line. From Facit southwards, the line was single-track — a legacy of the constrained times when the first part of the branch was built. Whitworth station, the next port of call, was a relatively simple affair; the single platform had a small goods yard opposite, in which a warehouse was situated on a looped siding. If Whitworth was considered as simple, I suppose Broadley might be viewed as being primitive, for it consisted of a platform with basic buildings and a flight of steps leading up to an over-line road bridge. A loop on the line doubled for passing purposes as well as for goods engines that were shunting wagons into the two sidings making up the goods yard.

Continuing south the remains of a couple of old sidings might be seen in the undergrowth, these being laid in during World War 2 to provide a loading facility for explosives traffic from a nearby factory. Next came the 105ft-high Healey Dell Viaduct. This structure comprised eight stone arches and one cast-iron span. Now no longer in use for railway purposes, it has the ignominious distinction of surviving to carry a main sewer from Whitworth. Shawclough & Healey station is encountered next. This station, like Britannia, was closed in 1917 due to staff shortages, although, unlike its near neighbour, it did reopen after the hostilities ended. A siding behind the station ran into serve an asbestos works, where traffic was so busy a private shunting engine was employed. Eventually the line reached Wardleworth, a suburb of Rochdale and in fact more conveniently located for the town centre than the station on the main line from Manchester to Leeds. Indeed, many Rochdale services were extended into Wardleworth as a means of convenience and as a way of relieving pressure on the main line station. It would be nice to think that trains might run here once again, but

Above:
Rawtenstall, today the northerly terminus of the preserved East Lancashire Railway, is enjoying something of a renaissance — based almost entirely on the new tourist industry generated by its railway. Who would have thought this to be the case 40 years ago, when it was just another struggling northern mill town that was about to slide into terminal decline as its traditional industries went in two decades of contraction. On 5 October 1953 Rawtenstall pilot 0-6-0 No 52549, from Bacup shed, approaches the station with a solitary brake van. Built by the L&YR as No 663 it was renumbered in 1909 as No 1051 then, as LMS No 12549, it spent many years at Bury and Bacup sheds on freight duties and was still at Bacup when the shed closed in 1954.
C. R. L. Coles

the Roch Viaduct leading to the town was blown up in 1972. It had been intended to demolish the viaduct anyway, but a freak occurrence during a test explosion saw the piers tumble down like dominoes. Finally the train would clatter over the points of Facit Branch Junction, pass the throat of the goods yard, then clatter once again as the points of the Oldham branch passed beneath the wheels. With a final burst of steam, the engine would pull through the massive goods yard complex and into the elevated station at Rochdale. Thus a journey (long since impossible) comes to an end, but for those who once travelled this way it will never be forgotten.

Services and Demise

It was always the ELR branch to Bacup that carried the bulk of the passenger traffic, but even this was never what might be termed as substantial. Yet there was a constant demand throughout the day, so that the two-coach trains were always well patronised. Railmotor services were experimented with between Bury and Bacup in 1906 but these were not fully introduced until 1914, and then only between Rawtenstall and Bacup. Seventeen trains a day were run, utilising railmotors made redundant on the electrification of the Holcombe Brook branch. Wartime economies saw the withdrawal of this service in 1915, and its reinstatement did not come until July 1919 when it had become a Ramsbottom-Bacup working. This became a home for the Hughes railmotors and the last of the stylish class was still employed here when it was withdrawn in 1948. Like Holcombe Brook it also saw the introduction of pull-push fitted 2-4-2Ts, of which three were allocated to Bury. The usual accompaniment for these engines was a converted railmotor coach which, by then, had seen far better days.

In February 1956 DMU sets were introduced and became an immediate success, despite a succession of mechanical failures. The service was extended and 35 trains were run each day between Bacup and Bury, with some workings extended through to Manchester. The trains were well patronised, reasonably reliable, and above all actually profitable. Yet Dr Beeching saw no future for commuter services outside London and he proposed the line's closure. Fortunately the Minister of Transport found the proposal too severe, and reprieved the line as far as Rawtenstall but the section on to Bacup was allowed to close in December 1966. Yet at least it fared much better than the Rochdale branch, which it must be said had always been viewed primarily as a goods line. For years services between Rochdale and Bacup had been operated by 2-4-2Ts, with often little more than a single coach to carry the passengers. It suffered the indignity of having its passenger service severely cut back during World War 1, then had it temporarily suspended during the 'fuel crisis' of 1947. It was never restored and, in the same year, Shawclough also lost its goods services. Broadley followed suit in 1952 and, with the exception of the Turners' Asbestos Siding, so too did Shawclough & Healey in 1964. Bacup closed entirely in December 1966, with the goods line being truncated to Rawtenstall, whilst on the eastern arm the line was cut back to Whitworth after the closure of Facit Goods Yard in 1963. Wardleworth lost its goods service in 1966 and what was left of the line from Rochdale finally succumbed in 1967.

The line from Bury to Rawtenstall remained open for coal traffic until final withdrawal of these trains in 1981. Upon closure the line passed into preservation as the East Lancashire Railway and has been progressively reopened north from Bury.

13 North From Halifax

Conception and Construction

As a prominent centre in the woollen textile trade, the town of Halifax had long seen itself as the most important commercial centre in Calderdale. Therefore, when the M&L main line bypassed the town, there was some feeling of outrage that a branch was not to be built immediately. Indeed a branch had been promised as early as 1841 but, for a further three years, the town's industrialists, traders and wool merchants had to make do with a horse-wagon service from Elland station. The civic fathers got more and more annoyed, whilst the carters and hauliers grew richer. On 1 July 1844 the town was finally to be connected by a branch from Greetland, but even this did not please many of the influential figures in the town. There were two specific difficulties with this branch; the direction in which it faced, and its steep gradients. Much of Halifax's traditional trading patterns was oriented westward up the Calder Valley and into Manchester, whilst the line as built had only an east-facing junction. This audacity was compounded by a 1 in 45 gradient, which in turn often defeated the inferior locomotives of the day, particularly when the rails were wet and greasy. Pressure was continually placed on the L&YR to rectify the situation and eventually a large triangular junction was built from Halifax down to the main line, with the opening of a curve from Dryclough Junction to Milner Royd Junction in January 1852.

Whilst this, coupled with a route to Bradford, may have seemed a satisfactory railway development, it takes no account of the way Halifax's textile industry developed. As mentioned in the introduction, this began with hilltop weaving communities located high on the Pennines close to the source of the wool crop. In most areas the weaving villages came to an end with the industrial revolution, when mills became established along supply routes in the valley bottoms. The primary reason for this migration was access to easily attainable supplies of coal, but at Halifax all the available sites soon became occupied. Accordingly the new development began to take place on the high ground west of the town, where new mills were supported by mines working a thin band of

Above:
With the arrival of the Great Northern Railway in Halifax, the original L&YR station at Shaw Syke was soon found to be inadequate. A series of improvements were introduced in the years that followed, but it was not until 1885 that a new joint station was built to serve the L&YR and the GNR. Three island platforms and a series of wonderfully ornate stone buildings presented visitors to the town with a more than fitting entrance but, in the years that followed, the station became a grim and gloomy hole situated inconveniently at the bottom of the town. In the late 1940s, the smoky atmosphere of Halifax station is captured as Class N5 0-6-2T No 5527 sits with a Queensbury train whilst an unidentified N1 0-6-2T stands at the far end of the island. *Gordon Coultas*

coal. This led to the demand for a connection to the railway network, which would also involve a line over the moors from Halifax to Keighley. Such a line was seen as the ideal means to provide satisfactory connections to the upland manufacturing communities like Holmfield, Queensbury, Denholme, etc. Accordingly, one of the prime movers behind the scheme was John Crossley, owner of what was then considered the 'world's largest carpet factory' at Dean Clough. Plans for a line submitted to Parliament were rejected in 1864, though an alternative scheme for a line of just 2½ miles was eventually approved.

The nominally independent Halifax & Ovenden Junction Railway was authorised on the understanding that the company had the backing of the GNR and L&YR. Work began at once, but it was soon found that the construction was going to be more demanding than had been initially envisaged. However, financial difficulties (despite the contribution of £30,000 each by the GNR and L&YR) were immediately evident due to the state of the money market which resulted in a poor take-up of the share offer. So the work was suspended, with the construction sites laying dormant. In the end, the H&OJR was jointly vested into the GNR/L&YR in 1870, a responsibility that was undertaken by the railway companies as a means of protecting their investment. Even so the line up to Holmfield was not going to be easily accomplished, as construction difficulties — including a massive landslide near Wade Street — would reveal. These prevented the opening between Halifax (Shaw Syke) and North Bridge until 1874. Goods traffic, particularly coal, was extensive from the outset.

However, the grand aim for a through line to Keighley kept resurfacing, with the Midland Railway being acclaimed alternately as the heroes or the villains of the cause. As the Midland pursued a railway across the moors, the company planned a bold venture to shorten the route between South Yorkshire and the Aire Valley. Throughout the 1860s the MR had been making allies with any railway that would help it achieve this goal — remember our discussions in the earlier chapters on Clayton West and Kirkburton. A link between Barnsley and Huddersfield, followed by a direct line to Halifax, with a final leg over the plateau to Keighley would in fact assure that end. Little wonder we hear of railway schemes entitled the Halifax, Huddersfield & Keighley Railway (rejected March 1864) or the West Yorkshire North & South Union Railway. The latter was a route conceived in 1876 by the engineer H. F. Foulton running from the Midland at Cudworth, and the GNR at Hemsworth, through Huddersfield and Halifax to join the Keighley & Worth Valley line at Haworth. In fact it was the Midland's withdrawal from the HHLR scheme that led the GNR to pledge an extension of its Bradford & Thornton line to Holmfield as we will discuss in the following chapter. In the meantime work on the

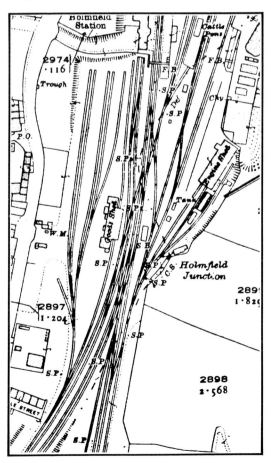

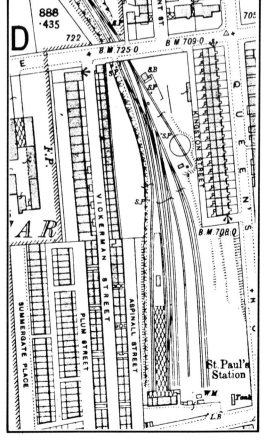

station. The textile manufacturing industries that grew up round (and those that migrated) here had initially thrived on the local coal, but as supplies became exhausted upwards of 75,000 tons of coal were being hauled up from the railway station by 1875. Whilst the branch line served immediate local needs, some speculators had envisaged it as being part of a grand trunk route to the north. As we discovered in Chapter six, the scheme only died due to the insolvency of the Hull & Barnsley Railway, but with its demise it firmly relegated the High Level's future to that of a secondary branch line.

The HHLR received Royal Assent on 7 August 1884, with much of its preamble being directly derived from the Hull & Barnsley & West Riding Junction Railway and Dock Act of 1882. The construction of the line is marked by two 'first' sod cutting ceremonies — one in November 1887 with the 'mayoral ceremony' coming three months later. One proposal, which could have spurred further development over the HHLR, was based on a plan put forward by the noted engineer J. E. Errington-Barnes towards the end of 1894. In the form of the Huddersfield, Midland & North West Central Railway, it proposed a line from Sheffield to Cononley, near Skipton, but it too came to naught. One positive outcome from all the development and proposed expansion was the construction of a superb L&YR/GNR joint station at Halifax in 1885.

The Line Described

Leaving the station at Shaw Syke a large viaduct had to be crossed to reach North Bridge, this was no less than 480yd long with spans of 36ft. Initially the railway facilities at North Bridge were confined to the goods yard, but a station was eventually opened here in March 1880. From there the railway began its assault on the steep escarpment leading up to the plateau, with an almost continuous 1 in 45 gradient. Clinging to the side of the valley as it climbed, the line curved round to Ovenden, encountering a succession of heavy and substantial earthworks. The first of these was 403yd tunnel at Woodside, followed by a six-arch viaduct at Lee Bridge and a further tunnel of 267yd at Lee Bank. Ovenden station was a modest timber-built affair which did not open until June 1881, and never had any permanent freight facilities. Beyond Ovenden the double-track ran due north to Holmfield, where engine shed facilities were provided.

From Holmfield the line to St Paul's ran south, crossing Shay Lane before entering Moorside Cutting beyond where the line entered the Wheatley Valley. A shallow cutting by Greystones Farm led onto the 10-arch Hebble Brook or Wheatley Viaduct. Climbing now on a 1 in 50 gradient, the line reached Wheatley Goods Yard where, despite

Above:

A series of difficulties with earthworks prevented the opening between Halifax (Shaw Syke) and North Bridge until 1874, and the rest of the route to Queensbury was not to open for a further five years — such was the difficult nature of the terrain that was to be encountered. On 23 April 1952 'N1' class 0-6-2T takes the 5.43pm train for Bradford through North Bridge, as a Halifax Joint Omnibus Committee Roe-bodied AEC double-deck bus crosses the bridge from which the station took its name. *Bryan S. Jennings*

section up to Ovenden continued, and the first trains were able to run through to Holmfield by late summer 1874 with goods services commencing on 1 September. The first passenger trains ran from Halifax to Queensbury on 1 December 1879, where connections were made into the Bradford-Thornton service.

The final link in the developing railway network to the north of Halifax was the Halifax High Level and North & South Junction Railway. Though quite a pretentious mouthful, this was only a relatively short branch from Holmfield to the Halifax suburb of St Paul's. Though little more than a mile from the town centre, St Paul's stood on a higher elevation, being well over 300ft (100m) above the main repeated pleas, the promised passenger station never materialised. In 1906, a well-used siding was provided at Wheatley into the Pennine Brewery of Messrs Webster & Co. Wood Lane was crossed by a substantial single masonry span, whilst a bridge over the footpath at Kitten Clough also benefited from magnificent stonework. Near Brackenbed Lane, massive retaining walls of around 70ft in height were to be noted.

At Pellon the booking offices were located on a wide over-line bridge, and these connected down to the island platform by means of a flight of steps. Timber-built waiting rooms and other sundry offices were covered by an attractive canopy of glass and ornamental iron-work. In later years the goods accommodation was extended at Pellon, including the provision of one road especially for use as a petrol and oil delivery siding. A large two-storey goods warehouse was erected from local stone, and provided with a substantial awning under which road vehicles might be loaded — a feature undoubtedly appreciated by generations of carriers using this shed during the eight month long Pennine winter! The line continued winding its way south through deep cuttings, many of which were spanned by substantial over-line bridges. The line entered St Paul's under one such structure carrying Hopwood Lane, where a wrought-iron girder bridge provided an excellent view of the station. The station was mainly laid out as a passenger terminus, but a massive area was levelled for the future provision of goods accommodation.

The station was provided with a 30ft wide island type platform with two faces, each 376ft long. Novel for this date, the platform was of reinforced concrete construction, despite the abundance of locally available sandstone. The buildings on the platform contained all the necessary station accommodation, whilst the whole facility was covered with a canopy of similar construction to that at Pel-

Left:
As the line up to Ovenden was originally built by an independent company, its construction was notoriously slow, with progress often depending on the state of available finances. Accordingly the line was taken over as joint operation between the L&YR and GNR, as is shown by the cast-iron notice plate at Ovenden station on 14 May 1955. With the driver and a young schoolboy looking towards the camera, Class N1 0-6-2T No 69464 drifts into the station's timber platform on a Bradford-Halifax working.
J. F. Oxley

Below left:
Long after the withdrawal of passenger services, the old cast-iron and glass canopy, which furnished the terminal station of the Halifax High Level Railway at St Pauls, stands decaying in the wind. The line's life was then centred round goods trains, and little use was made of the platform roads, except for the loading of consignments of biscuits and chocolate bars. In 1951 Sowerby Bridge-based Aspinall 0-6-0 No 52400 stands in the yard at the head of a rake of empty coal wagons.
The late Frank Alcock

lon. Both sets of canopies were provided by the firm of R. Hird & Co, of Shipley. A flight of steps led up to Aspinall Street, so-named in view of the L&YR's connection with the district. No shed was provided for the engines that worked the branch, as these were stabled at Holmfield. However, for ease of operation an ash/inspection pit and a manually operated turntable were provided adjacent to Kingston Street. This street was so named as it provided housing for workers at the nearby Kingston Confectionery Works and the Kingston Biscuit Factory; if this name is not widely known, then the nearby Mackintosh Street reveals the continuing connection between Halifax and what is now the firm of Rowntree Mackintosh (now part of the Nestlé multi-national). Yet, despite all the traffic this company put on to the railways, along with that of nearby textile mills, etc, the goods facilities at St Paul's were quite meagre, being limited to just four dead end sidings. No goods shed was forthcoming, nor was the simple provision of a yard crane.

Services and Demise
The first coal train on the HHLR ran on Tuesday 1 July 1890, with many passengers riding 'unofficially' on top of the loaded wagons. Yet the first official passenger train was that of 23 July when the directors invited local businessmen and civic leaders to travel the line. Coal services began on 1 August 1890 but, as the track needed time to consolidate, the passenger service could not be commenced until Thursday 4 September. On this date two special GNR trains were employed: one was made up of a tender engine, two brake thirds, four saloons and one composite; the other was a tank engine with two brake thirds and six composite coaches. At the entrance to Wheatley Tunnel the directors had the St Paul's stationmaster, Tom Oldham, present the Mayoress with a silver key which

Left:
The first trains were able to run through to Holmfield in the late summer of 1874, with passenger trains running from Halifax to Queensbury on 1 December 1879. When this service was axed on 23 May 1955, the average number of passengers on an off-peak journey was in single figures. With the complete closure of the line north of Holmfield, this meant that the only real use of the line was the carriage of coal up to stations on the High Level. One such working is pictured at Wheatley on 1 June 1960 with only a single wagon and guard's van making up 'Austerity' No 90122's load.
Gavin Morrison

The working of the High Level at this time was a pretty free and easy arrangement; loads were never great and trains were often worked without a guard's van. Some were pulled, others were propelled, as life on the weed-strewn High Level became part of a different world. On 29 June 1960 the old order finally comes to its end as Class 5MT 4-6-0 No 45339 shunts at Holmfield Yard. *Gavin Morrison*

Below left:
Despite its huge warehouse, Pellon no longer managed to generate sufficient traffic to keep the line open. Within three weeks of the photograph even coal traffic will be centralised at the Church Street and North Bridge goods yards down in Halifax town centre. The reason given for the withdrawal of the service was the fact that the traffic no longer justified the costs of maintaining the line — it had become a transport dinosaur in the age of the motor lorry. *Gavin Morrison*

Bottom left:
The final goods train from Holmfield ran on 29 June 1960: No 45338 collects the last three empty mineral wagons at Holmfield. Driver Harry Bell, Fireman Hollas of Sowerby Bridge and Guard Irvine Sykes must have felt a tinge of regret leaving Holmfield station for the last time, its glass and iron canopy and lattice footbridge decaying reminders of the long gone passengers who once travelled this way. Only the demolition trains would come now, so the old order and the grand dream of a main line to Scotland would finally fade and pass into oblivion as the next view shows. *Gavin Morrison*

unlocked a barrier across the portal and thus declare the tunnel open.

As we outlined earlier, the lines to Holmfield and St Paul's were taken over by the GNR and L&YR as a joint service. However, in view of the practicality in running passenger services from Halifax beyond Holmfield to Bradford or Keighley, it was decided that the GNR should handle this traffic. The L&YR concentrated on goods services from Halifax, which formed the bulk of the movements, though GNR did bring in substantial levels of traffic via Queensbury. Initially services on the High Level line to Queensbury were well supported, with 11 trains per day, except Sundays. However, by the end of the century the Class C12 4-4-2Ts were often down to a single-coach train, as passengers rapidly defected from the service in favour of tramcars. In terms of those wishing to go to Halifax this was quite understandable, for the half-hour journey was too slow and poorly timed to be of any real value. Consequently the bulk of passengers were those going to Holmfield, Queensbury or beyond — as might be imagined, these were not great in number. As a consequence the line was ripe for the enforced cut-backs which had to be applied to the railways during the locomotive and staff shortages of 1916-17. The passenger services therefore ended on the High Level line on 6 December 1916, whilst those on the Halifax-Queensbury service are more fully described in the following chapter.

Even though the regular passenger workings had gone, through coaches and sometimes full trains were worked from the High Level line at the local 'wakes' and on Bank Holidays. However, like similar services over the Stainland and Rishworth branches, this traffic ended in 1939 and never apparently resumed. A special working was noted with the running of an SLS/MLS railtour over the line on 5 September 1953, when Class N1 0-6-2T No 69487 pulled a four-coach train over the line. It was goods traffic that had become the line's staple diet and during 1917-18 this increased considerably, particularly coal inwards and khaki cloth and army rations (from the biscuit works) outwards. After the war this settled down to a basic three train daily service, one on Saturdays and none on Sundays. Quite often these were in the hands of L&YR 0-6-0 'A' class types, but Horwich-built 0-8-0s and GNR/LNER types were more than frequent visitors. The limit for trains on the steeply-graded line was 30 ordinary wagons and a brake van (not less than 15 tons). This continued as a basic pattern until the mid-1950s, but the closure of the Queensbury lines was to affect the line's viability. Having axed off the lines north of Holmfield, BR turned its attention the H&OJR and HHLR — stating that it intended to centralise coal distribution at the Church Street and North Bridge yards in Halifax.

Below:

Having travelled to Holmfield with my camera, it was soon apparent that there were very few locations that had a railway look about them today. Even the site of the station had given way to an industrial estate. This view, taken looking towards Holmfield, is indicative of what 30 years of decay can result in. Admittedly, the Halifax & Ovenden and Halifax High Level schemes were adventurous and perhaps some of the worst cases of optimism in the period of railway mania, but they were well-built and deserved a better fate than they received.
Author

On 17 May 1960 the announcement was made regarding the closure of the route to St Paul's and, despite the protestation of coal merchants and local industrial concerns, the last train ran on 27 June 1960 when a 'Black 5' 4-6-0 off Sowerby Bridge shed ran to collect the last rake of empty wagons that had been left at the former terminus. The suddenness took many local enthusiasts by surprise, and the local paper recorded that only a handful of children playing nearby were there to pay 'last respects' to the demise of yet another grand dream. The very last bit of the potential main line to Scotland, the short section from Halifax station to North Bridge Goods Yard, finally closed on just short of its centenary in 1974 — appropriately enough its end came on April Fool's day. Since closure parts of the line have disappeared, most notably the long viaduct between Halifax station and North Bridge which was demolished in the early 1980s, whilst the trackbed at North Bridge station is used to provide the foundation for one of the piers of Halifax's new road bridge. Elsewhere, however, it is still possible to trace the long-abandoned line as it follows the contours of the Pennine valleys.

14 The Queensbury-Keighley Line

Conception and Construction

The line west from Bradford on to the plateau beyond Clayton was conceived by a group of local businessmen, prominent among whom were the Fosters of the famous Black Dyke Mills, Queensbury. Their vision was for an independent line from Bradford to Keighley via Queensbury and Thornton, but it was later realised that the extension beyond Thornton would be both difficult and expensive to construct. As a result it was the Bradford & Thornton Railway Act that received Royal Assent on 24 July 1871. This authorised 5½ miles of railway from St Dunstan's (on the line between Bradford Exchange and Laisterdyke) to Thornton. This proposal was contemporary with the Halifax-Keighley scheme discussed in the previous chapter which, it seemed, would be absorbed by the mighty Midland Railway. Accordingly, to protect its territory, the Great Northern Railway decided to step in and take-over the Bradford & Thornton. This was sanctioned in an Act dated 18 July 1872.

The GNR's refusal to do anything to link Queensbury with Halifax and Keighley angered the local businessmen to such an extent that they decided once more to go their own way and promote a railway from Ovenden to Keighley. At this time the H&OJR was still in the making, but of course its completion would provide most of the vital link into Halifax. Their plan eventually became known as the Thornton & Keighley Railway and was authorised by an Act dated 5 August 1873. In the meantime the GNR had undergone a change of heart, and realised that, as it was committed to railway building in the area anyway, it might as well ally itself to the new scheme. Better this than chance incursions into the district by the Midland who, in 1873, were once again promising to build the Halifax-Keighley line if the GNR backed out. However, whilst the GNR had finally become 'committed' it decided it wanted nothing whatsoever to do with the Halifax-Huddersfield proposals, and so that piece of the 'grand plan' was allowed to die a natural death.

Work began on the Bradford-Thornton line on 21 March 1874 and, within a short time, it had reached Great Horton, allowing the opening of this section for goods traffic on 4 December 1876. Work progressed quickly westwards, allowing the commencement of freight service to Clayton by 9 July the following year. However, by now the GNR's financial position was at one of its lowest ebbs ever, and a notable slow-down was evident at the construction sites. This led the GNR to invite the Midland to inspect the works view to persuading them to undertake a joint operation of the line. The Midland officers travelled over the line from Halifax to Thornton in June 1878, as well as being conveyed by horse-cab to view the works on the

Below:
Visitors to Keighley station today would probably not associate the branch platforms (Nos 3 and 4) with anything other than the Worth Valley Railway's preserved steam trains, yet, for most of their life, these platforms saw dual use. As the signs in this picture on 19 February 1955 clearly show, these platforms were used for both Worth Valley and London & North Eastern trains. Services on both the ex-LMS and ex-LNER routes shared the Worth Valley line for a short distance on departure from Keighley. After arriving with the 2.31pm train from Bradford Exchange, the fireman takes the head lamp off Class N1 No 69464 before it crosses the coaches over to No 3 platform road and runs round the two-coach train. *J. F. Oxley*

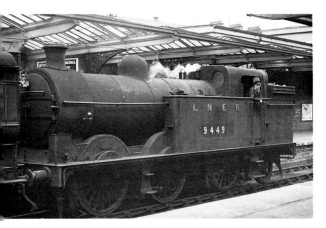

Keighley extension. Though impressed by what they saw, the Midland declined the invitation on account of their own financial worries. So the GNR pressed on alone, opening the line from Bradford to Thornton to passenger traffic on 14 October 1878. Freight had been commenced some six months earlier, but work on the passenger stations still had to be carried out at that time. As it was, Queensbury station was not completed until some considerable time later — and then only temporary platforms were provided.

Meanwhile, heavy civil engineering was required on the Holmfield-Queensbury line, not least of which were the massive Strines Cutting and the Queensbury Tunnel. The latter was 1 mile 741yd long. Even so, work was not unduly protracted considering the terrain and goods traffic began on 14 October 1878, whilst passenger services commenced on 1 December 1879. The Keighley section also had problems, and legislation was required in 1880 and 1881 to gain extensions of time. Work was notoriously slow, with landslips, bad weather and hard rock all conspiring to cause delays. A series of cuttings, where the earth slips were at their worst, were eventually replaced with two short tunnels with reinforced side walls. Goods trains began running from Thornton to Denholme on 1 September 1882 and Keighley on 1 April 1884. Passenger traffic development was a little more staged, with the Bradford-Thornton trains being extended to Denholme on 1 January 1884. By 7 April that year services had got to Ingrow (East) and, finally, into Keighley by 1 November. A welcome product of the scheme was the GNR's decision to ask the Midland for the joint development of a new station at Keighley which, when completed, resulted in a convenient interchange between passengers on the Queensbury route, the Midland main line and the Keighley & Worth Valley Railway.

The Line Described

From St Dunstan's the line passed through a mixture of residential and industrial areas, often necessitating substantial civil engineering and a number of over-line road bridges — including the tunnels at Ripley Street (85yd) and Manchester Road (312yd). Manchester Road and Horton Park stations provided passenger accommodation on this section, the latter being particularly busy when football or cricket matches were being played at the nearby Park Avenue ground. Great Horton was better known for its goods traffic, however, which was predominantly centred on wagon loads of baled wool handled at a large warehouse. At Great Horton the goods-only line to City Road diverged.

The City Road branch was some 1¼ miles in length and was double-track throughout. The line was opened in 1876 and was, throughout its exis-

Top:
A similar arrival is also pictured at platform No 4 on 17 October 1946 after 'N1' class 0-6-2T No 9449 arrived with a Saturday morning train from Queensbury. Today a different type of steam engine would be pictured here, probably one with a gleaming and resplendent finish, a living museum piece. Yet, for many, the grimy appearance of this LNER loco will capture the real face of Pennine railways. *H. C. Casserley*

Above:
Perhaps one of the least photographed features of the Queensbury line was where it tunnelled below the Worth Valley branch in order to attain the GNR goods yard in Keighley. Whilst the two companies enjoyed a more or less harmonious share of a joint passenger facility, there was no love lost when it came to goods traffic — then considered the staple diet of the railway. The tunnel was built basically as a cut and cover operation, but was still well executed and this 1958 picture pays tribute to the craftsmen who constructed it. Today, the goods yard beyond is the home of a Yorkshire Electric depot. *David Ibbotson*

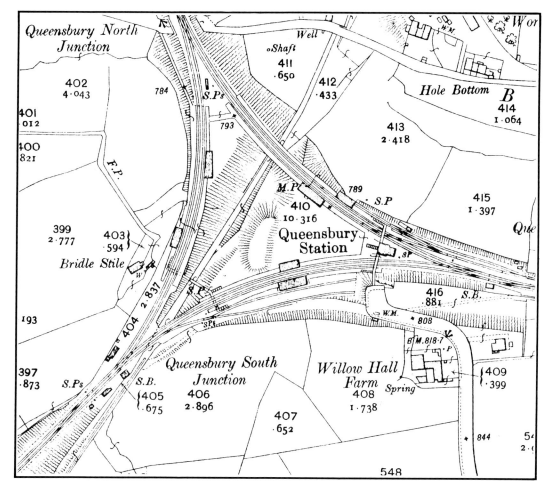

tence, a freight-only line. An extensive range sidings was constructed at the Great Northern's City Road depot, adjacent to Thornton Road, which catered for a wide range of general merchandise, in particular coal and freight for the many textile mills in the area. Prior to the line's opening, it had been the focus of proposals for a link line through to the Midland Railway's line to Forster Square. The line would have then extended westwards through Queensbury and on to Lancashire. The bill for this imaginative — and expensive! — scheme was, however, thrown out by parliament.

The next section out to Clayton was rural by comparison, but this contained a massive embankment near Pasture Lane which was 950yd long and over 60ft deep. Clayton boasted an island platform and a small, but extremely active, goods yard. The 1,057yd tunnel beyond Clayton was the next obstacle to be encountered on the route to Queensbury. Temporary platforms at Queensbury were eventually completely replaced by a massive triangular junction station in 1890. Six platforms were provided and, with a signalbox at the end of each point of the triangle, the station was unique. Along with Ambergate near Derby, it was the only British station to have platforms on each leg of a triangular junction at this time. (Although both Queensbury and Ambergate have subsequently declined in status, recent additions to the station at Shipley have created a third triangular station.)

Sadly Queensbury station was some distance from the town it purported to serve and it was always the intention to construct a tramway or a railmotor operated branch line up the hillside into the town centre. However, for some inexplicable reason the railway and town board (council) were at great variance over this proposal and applications were repeatedly refused. A rope-worked colliery waggonway ran under the station, and it was intended to link this to the railway, but once again the plans came to nothing. On the route to Holmfield, just beyond the station the line passed through Queensbury Tunnel, which was the longest tunnel on the GNR until 1910. During winter months this

Right:
Perhaps less well-known than its near neighbour on the Worth Valley line, Ingrow East is seen to good effect in this 1958 view. With only a few years left before even the last lingering goods service is withdrawn on 28 June 1965, the station still looks immaculate three years after passenger services ended. In many ways Ingrow East was a more attractive station than its nearby neighbour on the Midland line, yet it was the latter station which was to survive and enjoy considerable improvement in recent years.
David Ibbotson

Below right:
The line over to Queensbury had a number of substantial works of civil engineering, including the 14-arch viaduct at Wilsden pictured here on 14 April 1955. With regular 'N1', No 69444, crossing over with a two-coach Bradford local under an angry sky, the weather threatens another of the infamous Pennine showers.
Gordon Coultas

Bottom right:
Queensbury will always be known for its (almost) unique triangular junction layout, which offered an interchange between trains from Halifax, Bradford and Keighley. It must have been a rather confusing arrangement for some passengers, as the GNR issued an edict for 'change for...' signs to be added to the station nameboards in 1890. One such sign is pictured on 14 April 1955 as 'N1' No 69449 arrives with the 4.46pm Bradford-Halifax train.
J. F. Oxley

notoriously wet bore suffered major problems from the formation of giant icicles, so in the severest of weather a light engine had to be kept in steam inside the tunnel overnight to prevent their formation. Next came Strines Cutting, which was hewn from solid sandstone for 1,033yd and to a depth of 59ft at its greatest point.

On the route from Queensbury to Keighley the line had to cross a narrow valley near High Birks, where a substantial 300yd long embankment had to be constructed across treacherous ground. Near here the fire-brick works of J. Morton & Co were served by a siding, which provided extensive business almost down to the closure of the line. Next came the crossing of the Pinch Beck Valley, which was accomplished by a 20-arch viaduct 300yd long and 120ft high. Immediately beyond the S-shaped viaduct came Thornton station, where the first passenger trains caused a major celebration. From here the line left its northwesterly course and headed almost due west before penetrating the watershed at Well Heads. Before actually entering the 662yd long Wellhead Tunnel, a siding was thrown off to serve another fire-brick works. After Wellhead the line encountered the 150yd long Hammer's Hill Tunnel, before it curved north through Denholme, the highest station on the GNR system. The line then turned north-northeast and ran through Doe Hill Tunnel and the two inverted arches before reaching Wilsden station. This attractive little facility was opened on 1 July 1886 to serve a village of the same name, even though this was a full two miles distant. The section beyond Denholme included the 17-arch, 123ft high Hewenden Viaduct and a smaller nine-arch viaduct.

Cullingworth came next, and here the GNR established a sizeable goods yard. During World War 2 it was used extensively for war-effort traffic including machinery for Russia. In 1941 a concrete works was established in a nearby quarry, where massive concrete beams and prefabricated sections were produced. Yet, strange to relate, in the post-war years BR seemed almost averse to handling the traffic the works generated. After Cullingworth the line (known to drivers as the Alpine route) ran northwest to Ellar Carr, but then it turned west once again and dived into Lees Moor Tunnel to pierce the Worth Valley watershed. This tunnel was almost one mile long, with a sharp curve to the north, and inside its headings the navvies worked in appalling conditions, mainly due to the fact that a spring was tapped during the construction period and three-quarters of a million gallons of water poured out each day.

The line emerged in the Worth Valley only a short distance from the MR branch to Oxenhope and clearly visible from it. It then ran parallel to the Worth Valley. More heavy engineering, including cuttings and bridges and a 46yd tunnel took the line back to civilisation which was encountered at the Keighley suburb of Ingrow, from where it was but a short distance into the town. Beyond Ingrow (where the GNR established a locomotive shed), the line divided. The passenger line joined the Worth Valley route and shared MR metals into Keighley, whilst the other tracks passed under the Worth Valley route to enter the GN's goods yard in the town.

Services and Demise

After the inauguration of passenger trains, the services between Bradford and Thornton numbered nine each day, whilst a further six went between Halifax and Bradford. The immediate affect of these services was the revelation of inadequacies in the existing stations at Halifax and Bradford, both of which had to be enlarged to handle the Queensbury trains which had, in effect, become the last straw. Yet by 1901 tram services had penetrated from Bradford out to Queensbury and, within three years, motorbuses were offering cheaper travel down to Keighley. World War 1 did not help either, for many services were cut back and Manchester Road station closed in 1915, largely a victim of competition from the municipal tram routes along Manchester Road. In the 1920s the General Strike drove more customers onto the buses, whilst the 1930s saw further traffic drained away by the Depression. Though the Class C13 4-4-2Ts and the Stirling Class J52 0-6-0Ts had been replaced by Class N1 0-6-2Ts, and the four-wheel and six-wheel coaches had been superseded by bogie stock, the passenger fall-off continued at alarming annual rates.

To arrest the decline the LNER experimented with the Armstrong Whitworth diesel-electric railcar in 1935, then, in 1944, GWR railcar No 14 was tried, but it had difficulties keeping its feet on the steep gradients. Yet even on nationalisation there were 24 trains a day leaving Bradford Exchange for Halifax and Keighley, whilst the Halifax-Keighley service enjoyed something of an increased patronage. There was still a through coach each day from Halifax to King's Cross, which conveyed the wool magnates of the area to London by connecting into the Pullman service from Bradford. Yet, it was (on paper at least) a loss-making line and without considerations for its social importance the newly-nationalised railways decided to rid itself of the liability. The culprit was purported to Queensbury Tunnel, but the figures quoted for the repair of this 'liability' have always seemed dubious. When BR decided it could save £49,000 per annum by axing the services, they vanished quicker than anything Beeching ever accomplished. The last passenger train headed by No 69471 ran on Saturday 21 May 1955, but excursion trains continued to run throughout the summer.

Right:

Right:

Queensbury was also popular with tourist trains; some started there and headed for the coast, whilst others arrived there from the industrial mill towns in order to allow passengers a ramble across the open moors. On Easter Monday 1920, excursions offered from Keighley and Queensbury included Cleethorpes, Skegness, Mablethorpe and Cromer (all good GNR destinations), whilst incoming trains arrived from Huddersfield (three), Leeds (two), Bradford (six) and Grantham (one). However, it is a very different train pictured at Queensbury in September 1948, as ex-GCR Class Q4 0-8-0 heads a breakdown train through the station.
David Ibbotson

Right:

As the service drew towards its finale the trains, once three or four coaches each, were often down to a single carriage, and even then it wasn't difficult to find a seat. On 14 April 1955 just five weeks before closure, Class N1 0-6-2T No 69434 rumbles through the deep cutting between Clayton and Great Horton, no doubt making light work of its short mid-day train. *Gordon Coultas*

The closures sparked off great controversy. Local opinion was particularly incensed by the continued operation of excursion trains over the line, given that the condition of Queensbury Tunnel was the ostensible reason for the line's closure.

But this was not the end of closures, for the following spring the Holmfield-Queensbury and the Cullingworth-Ingrow sections were closed to freight traffic. Although these closures were effective from May 1956, the lines remained in place for a short while. Sadly, a grand suggestion debated in Parliament that proposed the reopening of the line to diesel railcars never came to fruition.

On the section beyond Ingrow the trackbed was relaid by BR in the spring of 1957, but this was not to form some reopening scheme. They were in fact laid to test Dowmac concrete sleepers, on which deliberate derailing tests were undertaken with Class G5 0-4-4T No 67338, two coaches and a bogie bolster wagon. Early in 1957 the line was in use again, this time as part of controversial 'fume-emission/cancer tests'. As part of the BTC diesel locomotive introduction and evaluation trials, it was decided that tests would have to be carried out to see what harmful gasses or emissions might be created when diesel engine fumes mixed with those from steam locomotives inside confined spaces. In conjunction with physicians from St Bartholomew's hospital in London, the gases produced by the combined emissions of diesel locomotives Nos D8010/8011 and 'A3' class No 60081 *Shotover* were measured and analysed. The results of these tests are not readily available, but it is known that the two diesels (later TOPS Class 20) were unable to contend with the Pennine weather and suffered from frozen radiators and cooling systems. Further tests took place on the line, when Derby Research Centre experimented with short-wave radio signals through the tunnels, whilst a prototype ballast cleaning machine built by Hunslet's of Leeds was evaluated at Great Horton station in 1959. In addition, the route was used regularly for training drivers to handle diesel locomotives and multiple units.

In August 1958 the down line was closed between Wilsden and Thornton, and it was duly used to store mineral wagons awaiting consignment to Shildon Works for repair or disposal. Goods traffic from the concrete works at Cullingworth continued to grow, but the non-availability of 50-ton wagons and the general unreliability of the BR service forced the company to switch to road haulage in 1963 — the goods yard then closed on 11 November that year. Thereafter, the freight service from Bradford terminated at Thornton, but even this was not to last as the trains dwindled to just two a week. The entire section from Horton Junction to Thornton closed on 28 June 1965. On the same date the last remaining stub at the northern end, that from Keighley to Ingrow East, also closed but, in its demise, it allowed the rebirth of the Keighley & Worth Valley Railway which was then afforded unrestricted access into the 'branch platforms' of Keighley station, unfettered by conflicting BR movements.

After the closure to Thornton, freight services continued to operate over the section from St Dunstan's to Great Horton and thence to City Road over the goods only branch. Even this traffic was, however, to be terminated with the final closure of the City Road yard on 28 August 1972 when the Class 08 trip working was withdrawn. The yard had been reduced to a coal depot only on 5 June 1967, when general freight facilities were withdrawn. The freight yard at Great Horton was also closed from 28 August 1972. Thus ending the history of the Great Northern's 'Alpine' routes to Keighley and Halifax.

Since closure much of the line has disappeared, particularly in Bradford where the Council received a grant in the early 1980s to landscape the cuttings (largely to solve problems with rubbish accumulation and rodents). It is still possible, however, to see distinct traces of the line within the city. Outside the city there is much more visible, with the viaducts at Thornton, Hewenden and Cullingworth still extant. Although threatened with demolition, a local campaign ensured the bridges were to survive — indeed there were even reports in the railway press that trains could reappear as part of a preservation scheme. At Queensbury, whilst traces of the triangular station remain, much has disappeared as part of a landfill scheme. For the railway historian searching after the remains of closed lines, the Queensbury routes offer a considerable amount of interest.

Right:
On the same day the engine works back to Keighley through Great Horton. By now the train has gained an extra coach which has been added at Bradford Exchange to cater for the additional Saturday evening traffic. The peak trains were still well-used, but this was not sufficient to save the line from closure. How much different the story would have been if the stations had been reduced to unstaffed halts and DMUs introduced. When DMUs were used over the route for driver training in 1956 it raised much hope locally that the services would be reintroduced. A hard winter had shown how much people needed the railway and these matters were raised in Parliament by a number of local MPs, but these hopes turned to anger when it was emphatically stated by the secretary to the Minister of Transport that 'the closure of the Halifax Bradford and Keighley Railway had been abundantly justified'. *J. F. Oxley*

Right:
Another location that took some finding today was the famous triangular station at Queensbury and, on the ground, it was difficult to find anything to photograph to really do justice to the subject. However, higher up the hill, a more distant view shows to good effect the location of the triangle. Can you spot it? It is dead centre in the picture, a white-banded mill chimney standing just above its top left-hand corner. If nothing else, this view taken from some distance below the town) illustrates just how far the station was from Queensbury. As a memory a nearby pub is still called The Junction — it serves a good pint too! *Author*

15 The Worth Valley Branch

Conception and Construction

In the following chapter we will discover the origins of the main line through Keighley, which was promoted in the guise of the Leeds & Bradford Railway. Whilst this line's arrival in March 1847 immediately brought additional prosperity to the area, it did little to benefit the Worth Valley. The way forward for that valley was seen in the promotion of a line across the moors from the Calder Valley. Some of the schemes with this in mind having been discussed in earlier chapters. One of the earliest ideas did not envisage the route going via Halifax, but rather promoted a link to the M&L at Hebden Bridge. Known as the Hebden Bridge & Keighley and Leeds & Carlisle Junction Railway, the 1845 proposal foresaw a massive bore being tunnelled beneath Oxenhope Moor, but at a cost of £350,000 this was never likely to attract sufficient investment.

Accordingly the Worth Valley had to wait a further 15 years, before serious proposals began to emerge once again. Yet the growing importance of Haworth, due to its literary connections, was attracting considerable numbers of visitors in a very early form of tourism. When John McLandsborough, a civil engineer from Otley, travelled to visit the home of the Brontës, he was disgusted to find an absence of railway communications. The Midland Railway, enjoying a monopoly over local rail-carrying capacity, on the other hand saw no necessity to do anything about the situation. Yet, in October 1861 they did promise to support the Keighley & Worth Valley Railway Bill, in which McLandsborough appeared as consulting engineer. The Bill became an Act on 30 June 1862 and the first sod was duly cut with great ceremony on Shrove Tuesday 9 February 1864. The line appeared an easy one to construct, but a 150yd tunnel below Halifax Road at Ingrow was to prove the first obstacle. Inside, the contractors encountered a bed of wet sand and, to provide a secure foundation, piles had to be sunk down to the bedrock. The combination of vibration and subsidence caused serious damage to a Methodist chapel above, which had to be rebuilt as a consequence. The contractor also had difficulties with labour, and he was fined by the company for failing to adhere to the terms of the contract. There is a story that the work was delayed because a cow ate the plans whilst they were left in a field near Oakworth in 1864, but this piece of history became more and more embellished as it became part of local folklore. On 1 November 1866 the contractor ran an engine to the terminus at Oxenhope, but plans that this would signal the line's completion were dashed just two weeks later when severe flooding washed away a 40yd long stretch of embankment near Damems. The track was left suspended across the gap, and work on rectifying this and other damage took until April. On Saturday 13 April 1867 a Midland tank engine ran a seven-coach train (and a luggage brake), in which invited dignitaries and guests were to travel. However, the first train came to an embarrassing halt on the 1 in 58 gradient due to greasy rails

Above:
With the GNR route recently closed to passenger traffic, the only widespread use of platform Nos 3 and 4 at Keighley station were the Worth Valley push-pull trains. By this time a good many of the mid-day workings were often just a single coach but, at peak times, two and three coaches were provided and, according to former Keighley booking clerk Phillip Stead, these were not always sufficient. In July 1958 Ivatt 2-6-2T No 41326 gets ready with a three-coach train. *Kenneth Field*

The Line Described

Whilst this book does not concern itself with preservation matters to any great extent, our description of the journey along the Worth Valley branch is based on a modern-day trip from Keighley up to Oxenhope. So come with me as we descend the long ramp leading down to Keighley's No 4 platform. At first there seems to be a bit of jostling as the mass of excited passengers congregate around the bottom of the ramp or by the refreshment stand, but soon space is found and the camera comes out. One of the line's immaculately preserved locomotives presently pulls into the station having come down the branch and, after running round its train, is soon ready to depart. The first thing we notice is the huge water tower, the platform having been extended out to this point in 1971. On the opposite side of the line, a turntable will be observed, some will know that it once stood on the moors at Garsdale Junction alongside the Settle & Carlisle line. Built for the Midland Railway by the Carlisle firm of Cowans, Sheldon, it had the distinction of later being enclosed within a stockade after high winds sent it spinning round and round whilst an engine was being turned.

Leaving Keighley the steep gradient is compounded by a sharp curve to the right, where the line passes the former Great Northern Goods Depot. Now used as a base for Yorkshire Electric, it still bears mute witness to the extensive traffic the GNR carried out of Keighley over the Queensbury lines. The junction for those lines is noted a little further on, but the single line connection that once left the Worth Valley line here has now been removed for well over a quarter of a century. The line soon reaches Ingrow station 1¼ miles from Keighley. The station building here came from Foulridge as we will discover in the next chapter. Its removal from the Skipton-Colne line was very much a team effort, with great assistance from employees on training programmes, but much of the work in overseeing its removal fell upon David Pearson. From the first rumblings about its removal in 1986, to its complete restoration, work progressed in a highly professional way. The completed structure and the associated carriage museum and *Bahamas* complex making a perfect visitor centre in their own right. Immediately beyond the station comes the short tunnel below Halifax Road, on the other side of which stands Clough's Mill — once furnished with its own private delivery siding.

Late in 1867 a small one-coach station opened at Damems, two miles from Keighley, with the intention of serving a nearby mill. More folk-lore suggests that its wooden crossing-keeper's shed was nearly taken away by a farmer who mistook it for a hen hut! The station was only used at peak times and it closed in May 1949, but it has since found a

Below:
A scene perhaps familiar with many visitors to the Worth Valley Railway today, but there are many subtle changes that have taken place since this 1952 view. Notable additions to the scene nowadays would include the former Garsdale turntable, which now stands a little distance to the rear of the water column seen in this view. Gone too are the push-pull carriage sets, as is the generally scruffy state into which the railway had been allowed to deteriorate in postwar Britain.
David Ibbotson

Bottom:
Descending the branch through Ingrow heading towards Keighley in May 1952, an unidentified Fowler 2-6-2T propels a two-coach set with the driver clearly seen in the leading end. Never quite in the same league as the GWR Auto-coaches, these sets always had an antiquated feel about them and did little to endear themselves to passengers of the day. *David Ibbotson*

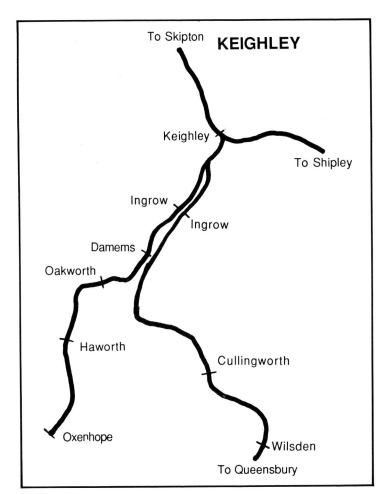

KEIGHLEY

To Skipton

Keighley

To Shipley

Ingrow

Ingrow

Damems

Oakworth

Haworth

Cullingworth

Oxenhope

Wilsden

To Queensbury

Right:
From this picture it will be clearly demonstrated that not all the Worth Valley trains were motor-worked, even though the push-pull sets were generally employed. In July 1950 Manningham-based 0-6-0 No 43784 pulls a three-coach train up through Ingrow. These '3Fs' were introduced by Deeley in 1906 and later rebuilt by Fowler with a Belpaire firebox. Weighing 46tons 3cwt, the type had a tractive effort of 21,010lb, more than enough for a Worth Valley passenger train.
David Ibbotson

Below right:
Famous for its starring role in the Lionel Jeffries film 'The Railway Children' was Mytholmes Tunnel. Its setting as the scene where an accident took place in the hare and hounds chase will probably always be remembered by the words 'Its awfully dark in here', yet reality shows that even the tunnel notice-board on the far side can be seen clearly due to the fact that it was just 75yd long.
David Ibbotson

new lease of life — not least with the provision of the small cabin from Earby Gates Crossing on the Skipton-Colne line. In 1971 the society decided that the straight section of line beyond Damems was just right for the construction of a passing loop and, after a period of hand signalling, it was furnished with a fully restored Midland Railway signal cabin from Frizinghall near Bradford. Oakworth has to be one of the jewels on the line, its period atmosphere creating the right setting for all those period scenes in films and television. Beyond the station the line passes over the three-arch Mytholmes Viaduct where it crosses the River Worth. Next comes Mytholmes Tunnel which was built to replace the timber trestle viaduct across the dam at Vale Mill. The contract was let in 1891 and, on 6 November the following year, the service was diverted through the tunnel. However, the viaduct was not demolished straight away, but was left in place until the tunnel had proved itself in service.

Haworth station, three miles from Keighley, is the centre-piece of the line. It was never very well situated for the town centre which lies quite some distance up the hillside, but a footbridge leading up to Haworth at the Oxenhope end of the station has the advantage of providing an ideal vantage point for photographers. To the other side of the bridge stands the gaunt stone goods warehouse, in which the society's first workshop was established. In 1979 work began on a new shed alongside the warehouse, much to the relief of all those who toiled to try and maintain the line's ageing fleet of locomotives. Another mile through attractive countryside take us up to the terminus at Oxenhope, where a goods shed and station building were available to the preservation society members. However, just a single coal siding was left to serve as the goods yard by then. So the volunteers had to lay in new facilities, including the 'white shed' built as an extension to the goods warehouse. This shed was originally intended as a locomotive depot, but its rôle was to develop as a carriage restoration shed and it was been given suitable extensions in the intervening years. A further building, the 'green

shed' was erected as a museum, and place in which to store locomotives that are out of service.

Services and Demise

Normal passenger services began on Monday 15 April 1867, with goods traffic commencing on 1 July that year. It seems as though the first trains were handled by a mixture of rebuilt, but nevertheless superannuated, tank engines such as the 0-6-0 and 0-4-2WTs. There were six trains daily, with two on Sundays, but this had altered to five passenger workings to Oxenhope and seven to Keighley by 1875. There were also three goods trains each day. As the century progressed, Johnson 0-6-0 half-cab tank engines came to the line, and No 1347 is reputed to have been one of the regulars. In 1883 five new 0-6-0Ts came to the area — Nos 218/19 and 1397-99 — and with full cabs they were considerably better for the crews working the Worth Valley line. By the end of the century the Brontë connection was bringing increasing numbers of passengers on to the 17 branch trains that ran each

day, particularly after the Brontë Museum opened in 1895. Around 1916 the Midland began experimenting with motor-fitted trains, and the line to Oxenhope was ripe for such development. Exactly when pull-push fitted 0-4-4Ts began working the Worth Valley branch is not confirmed, but they are certainly in evidence in photographs taken just after the end of World War 1.

In the LMS era, the ex-Midland types were replaced with motor-fitted Ivatt 2-6-2Ts based at Bradford's Manningham shed. These locomotives included Nos 41273 and 41325/26. Fowler 2-6-4Ts were also employed, though Derby-built stalwarts such as the Class 3F 0-6-0s were still regularly rostered on the goods services. Tender locomotives were not widely employed on the branch passenger services, as the head-shunt at Oxenhope was too short for most types. In the end the head-shunt was to be extended by the preservationists in 1971, thereby allowing not only one but two engines to run-round at the same time. One of the most common tender engines seen on passenger duties in BR days, on trains such as excursions and holiday specials, were Hughes 2-6-0 'Crabs' and smaller types like the Ivatt 2-6-0s. As part of the streamlining process needed to attempt to save the branch, the passenger services went over to DMU operation on 13 June 1960. However, despite this last ditch effort, the local Transport User's Consultative Committee decided that, whilst some hardship would be occasioned by withdrawal, the line should close to passengers at the end of 1961. The case against closure had been hard fought by Keighley Council but, in the end, the trends were just too hard to fight. With the ever-growing decline in passenger numbers, opponents of closure faced the fact that the last train would run on Saturday 30 December 1961.

Rebirth

When the last train left Keighley at 11.15pm it was packed to capacity and, in view of the special occasion, it was decided that return tickets would be issued. Normally the train would have worked back down the valley as 'empty coaching stock'. Few on board that night would have thought it possible that anything else could be in store, for even the goods services were scheduled for withdrawal six months later. However, inspired by the death of the Queensbury lines, and determined that the same should not happen in the Worth Valley, a Mr R. G. Cryer called a meeting at Keighley's Temperance Hall in May to discuss ways of preserving the line. A provisional preservation society committee was elected, with Mr Cryer as the Chairman. His group then acted very quickly, establishing the foundations that would ensure that the line was not torn up when BR finally closed it. On 23 June 1962

Right:
**Before 'The Railway Children'
came, this was the sort of
scene common at the stations
on the branch. On 3 June 1960
a two-coach set is worked up
towards the terminus by Ivatt
2-6-2T No 41326 from
Manningham Shed (55F).**
Gavin Morrison

Below right:
**A year earlier it is sister engine
No 41325 that has come up the
branch to arrive at the neat
little terminus of Oxenhope.
Story has it that during the
dark days of World War 2, a
group of squaddies was issued
travel permits to Oxenholme,
but the name of the Worth
Valley terminus was
inadvertently inserted on to the
travel warrants instead. Phillip
Stead recalls the event, as the
men travelled up on the last
train on a Friday night along
with a group of sailors who
were going on leave. A fight
broke out on the train and the
men were ejected at the
terminus, when it was realised
that they had arrived at the
wrong place the soldiers tried
to get back on board but the
guard wasn't having any of that
as his train was due to work
back empty stock. Having rid
himself of the trouble-makers,
he reported the incident to
Stead at Keighley but, to this
day, no-one has any idea of
how the soldiers got to their
correct destination — or do
they?** *Gavin Morrison*

Right:
**The transformation from state-
run branch line to one run by
enthusiasts was quite amazing
and, no matter how many
preserved railways follow, the
Worth Valley can always claim
to be amongst the first to take-
over a standard gauge British
Railways line. Events over the
past 25 years have been quite
spectacular, but few will be as
evocative of those early days
when it all began to happen.
Such an early event is pictured
on 11 April 1967, with a variety
of activities taking place in
Haworth Yard.** *Gavin Morrison*

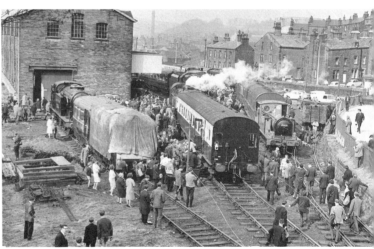

the withdrawal of the freight service was marked by a six-coach preservation society special, from Bradford (Forster Square) to Oxenhope behind Midland '3F' 0-6-0 No 43586. Unfortunately, this engine met its end later that year, but the society went on from strength to strength. So, too, has Bob Cryer; he is now the Labour MP for Bradford South.

By 1964 the Preservation Society had finally convinced BR that it was a serious and credible organisation and, in due course, permission was granted for them to store some of their locomotives and carriages at Haworth Goods Yard. The first to arrive (on the back of a Pickfords low-loader) was ex-L&YR 'Pug' No 51218 whilst the next, *Sir Berkeley*, also came by road about two weeks later. The collection of museum pieces slowly grew, attracting more than a passing interest from those who visited Haworth because of its connection with the Brontës. As the scheme began to gather pace, it

was decided to put the matter on a proper business footing and the Keighley & Worth Valley Light Railway Ltd was formed in February 1966. In 1967 the new company completed the formal agreement with BR allowing them to purchase the entire line for £45,000, with the exception of Platform No 4 at Keighley station which had to be leased. In due course a Light Railway Order was obtained, permitting the line to be reopened on 29 June 1968. At 2.35pm that day a double-headed train, in the hands of tank engines Nos 41241 and 30072 pulled a six-coach train out of Keighley.

In so doing, it became the first British Railways line in the area to become preserved and, in the years that have followed, it has become (in many ways) a 'market leader' in the field of preserved railways. At four miles in length it is not as long as some, nor does it want to be — it has found its 'niche market'. As even non-railway enthusiasts will tell you, the Keighley & Worth Valley Railway has since gone on to become the setting for many television and film settings, but the most memorable of all of these has to be the film adaptation of E. Nesbitt's *The Railway Children* made in the 1960s. Bernard Cribbins, Lionel Jefferies, Dinah Sherridan and Jenny Aguter brought to life that charming tale of childhood days of a century ago. With that memory we will leave the Worth Valley, recommending all who want to know more about its preservation days to take a journey along the branch.

Above left:
With the growing support of an enthusiastic band of volunteers, the Worth Valley Railway has managed to progress considerably. Major restoration schemes have come to fruition and even more ambitious schemes have been undertaken; for example, as the book goes to press it is noted that the volunteers' hostel at Haworth has recently been completed, providing quite luxurious accommodation for those who come from afar to work the railway. Much, as always, depends on the resources available to the preservationists, but pride has never been lacking as illustrated by the turn-out of Stanier '8F' 2-8-0 No 48431 pictured at Keighley as it waits to back on to its train in 1984.
Keighley & Worth Valley Railway

Left:
However, there are some projects you would have never believed possible. For example, I had seen Standard Class 2MT 2-6-0 No 78022 at Woodham Brothers' scrapyard in Barry on 4 April 1975, just before the Standard Four Group removed the rusting hulk to Haworth. In the years that followed thousands of pounds and millions of man hours went in to restoring No 78022, but it was a proud team who saw her roll out of the shed on Friday 16 October 1992. I was privileged to be there to witness it. *Author*

16 The Midland Branches to Colne and Barnoldswick

Conception and Construction

Despite its apparent central position in the North Lancashire industrial conurbation, the textile manufacturing town of Colne had always enjoyed strong trading links with towns in the Aire Valley. This trading pattern had substantially developed with the advent of the Leeds-Liverpool Canal, which fully opened in 1816. This one significant event proved to be the catalyst for massive industrial development, as it provided an efficient and reliable method of transporting coal and raw materials to the new factories, and an efficient means by which products could be consigned to the ever growing market. The Aire Valley was ripe territory for a railway, but a spate of early proposals came to nothing and it wasn't until the opening of the Leeds & Bradford Railway in 1846 that the first important steps were taken in this direction. Welcomed though the Leeds-Liverpool Canal had been at its outset, three decades on it was seen as a slow and outmoded means of transport when to the newly industrialised region 'time meant money'.

During the promotion of the L&BR it was decided that an extension would be taken to Keigh-

ley, but this was soon superseded by a plan for a line to Skipton, which in turn had become a proposed railway to Colne by the autumn of 1844. A double junction was made at Shipley and the railway opened to Keighley in March 1847, with a single line of rails reaching Skipton by September. Colne was to come next, but in the event this opening was yet some time away. The Leeds & Bradford Extension Railway were not holding back with the construction and, to many observers, the line appeared to be nearing completion by the spring of 1848, but services were not to start yet. The reason for this is lost in the railway politics of the era, but when one considers the involvement of the infamous 'Railway King' George Hudson this is not surprising. In an effort to prevent the M&L acquiring the L&B, Hudson had promised to pay the latter company's shareholders a dividend of 10% per annum. However, the Midland could see little way of justifying the payment whilst Colne was the dead-end of a line from Skipton — the company's eager expectation was the arrival of the East Lancashire Railway from Accrington which would then provide a through route to the North Lancashire

Right:
Ex-L&YR No 50621, which was later preserved, waits at Skipton with the 4.30pm service to Barnoldswick on 2 June 1952. *Harold D. Bowtell*

Far right:
Stanier-designed 2-6-4T No 42475 is pictured at Earby station on a northbound train for Skipton. On the platform, passengers make their way towards the Barnoldswick branch train. It is salutory to think that, by the time the children featured reached maturity, that the passenger service along the Barnoldswick branch would be but a memory. *Real Photographs/Ian Allan Library*

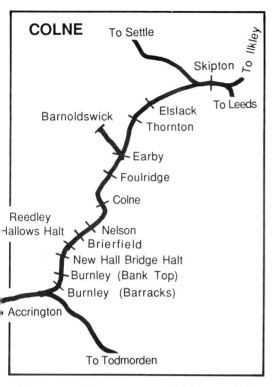

COLNE

To Settle

To Ilkley

Skipton

Elslack

To Leeds

Barnoldswick

Thornton

Earby

Foulridge

Colne

Reedley
Hallows Halt

Nelson

Brierfield

New Hall Bridge Halt

Burnley (Bank Top)

Burnley (Barracks)

Accrington

To Todmorden

paper commenting 'the (Midland) railway could have instituted a service upon their line of rails some months ago, but saw no necessity to do so until the line of the Lancashire Company was upon Colne. This lack of promise reflects bad upon the promoters of the railway, betraying the trust of investors and future customers alike'.

The flow of traffic from the branch was considerably weighted in favour of the Aire Valley, as is testified to by the construction of the Barnoldswick branch. Authorised by an Act of Parliament in 1867, work on the line was completed in time for an opening — to what was then a Yorkshire town — on 8 February 1871. The significant thing was the way in which its traffic flow was envisaged, as being evidenced by the fact that the junction pointed in the direction of Skipton. The branch had not been a difficult one to build and, from the outset, it was to be worked by the Midland Railway — probably one of the farthest flung outposts from Derby imaginable, perhaps not in distance but certainly in life-style.

The Line Described

From Skipton the line heads southwest, and about half a mile from the station, a major junction was established in 1850 with the divergence of the 'little' North Western Railway line to Lancaster. In turn this line was to see a further expansion in traffic when the famous Settle & Carlisle line opened in 1876, providing a new main line route to the northwest and Scotland. From the modern Skipton by-pass you can still see the junction, with the route to Carlisle curving away to the right, but only a green swathe exists to the left. When it was a railway, the line was carried by embankments over the

mill towns and (more importantly) Liverpool. Yet there was to be some prestige in reaching Colne first and, with the ELR being beset by problems, the Midland reached Colne in October 1848. A planned join-up had been intended for the end of the year, but further difficulties on the ELR prevented this from happening, so the Midland's delaying tactic slightly rebounded on them. A local

Above:
At the very end, the Barnoldswick passenger services had deteriorated to a level that was little more than a morning and early evening working taking students to the grammar school at Skipton or schools and colleges in Keighley. There was even a Saturday morning service, for the Grammar school still had classes then (albeit optional). Usually the pull-push service was operated by a fitted '84xxx' class, quite often one that came all the way from Leeds. In the end BR priced the traffic off the rails by refusing to issue scholar's tickets, and six motor coaches had to be employed to take the train's place — today a bottle-bank stands where trains once ran. *Paul D. Shannon*

low-lying ground to a crossing of the River Aire, beyond which a further set of embankments led it to the shoulder of Elslack Moor. Two substantial cuttings, joined in the middle by a short tunnel (which was in effect a covered carriage drive) took the line past a palatial country residence near Broughton. After this the line ran parallel with a more ancient transport route, a Roman road, but at a much lower level as the railway dived into yet another cutting. An embankment came next, with a bridge across a stream, but the railway then did the unthinkable (and upsetting antiquarians of the day to boot) it carved through the site of the Roman Fort near Elslack station. Two more cuttings gave way to another embankment, beneath which the route of the Pennine Way would eventually pass as it descended from Elslack Moor to Thornton in Craven, where the station closed to goods trains as early as 1951. A more southerly curve took it down to the town of Earby.

Earby was of little industrial consequence when the railway arrived, having been by-passed by the canal, but it had substantially developed when the line eventually closed. Though the line eventually met its Waterloo, the signalbox from here has survived thanks to the Keighley & Worth Valley Railway, who subsequently installed it at Ingrow Cross-

ing. South of the station, and just beyond the point where the railway crosses Earby Beck, the Barnoldswick branch diverged. Leaving the main line for a short while we will head along the branch, curving west to recross the beck before running in a northwest direction. Near Salterforth the line went through a deep cutting before running downhill to cross the Leeds-Liverpool Canal on the skew. Into the terminus the train would roll, a prim building of stone adorning the single platform, but its appearance spoilt by wooden extensions on either side. By the time I made my only visit to Barnoldswick station in June 1966, which by then was served by goods trains only, the whole place had an air of neglect about it, but this is hardly surprising as the line closed completely the following month.

Rejoining the main line, the double-track sped south passing under the road to Barnoldswick before coming out of a cutting on to a section of embankments and underline bridges. Near Accornlee the line started to take a more westerly course to reach Foulridge, where a high ridge of land had been tunnelled to provide a course for the canal. This was some of the most difficult terrain faced by the builders of the railway, but here they built an attractive little station to serve both the industrial customers and an important agricultural community. The station at Foulridge was closed and abandoned on 5 January 1959 and here it stood for many years slowly depreciating but, like the signalbox from Earby, it too was to find a new lease of life on the Keighley & Worth Valley Railway. We have already met the building in the previous chapter where it poses as the new Ingrow station. It is not quite historically correct, but does this really matter, the splendid restoration of a piece of Midland architecture on a preserved Midland Railway branch line is satisfying to all but the purists. Finally, from Foulridge the line takes a huge curve and follows a heavily engineered course into the town of Colne where it would eventually meet up with the ELR.

Services and Demise
In some ways it is difficult to separate the services operated on both of the Colne branches, as many of these were through workings. Indeed one fellow historian urged me to keep the two accounts as one, but in the end it was decided to present a separate, though brief account of services on the Skipton-Colne and Barnoldswick lines. From the outset there was a degree of joint working on the two Colne branches and you were probably more likely to see an ELR (later L&YR) locomotive on the passenger services than one of Midland origin. The Barnoldswick branch was exclusively worked by the Midland and several trains actually ran beyond

Above:
Foulridge station, the building from which much later was to be rebuilt at Ingrow, is seen on 5 June 1952 with 2-6-4T No 42549 approaching on a three-coach stopping train. The line was never very busy with local traffic, although it was not a large loss-making service in its own right. Where it did show a profit was in its use as a vital cross-country service between northwest Yorkshire and north Lancashire. Strangely such values were never taken into consideration when assessing the viability of a route. Today, passengers from Accrington, Burnley or Colne who want to spend a day in Skipton would have to travel via Leeds or Lancaster to do so! *Oliver F. Carter*

Above left:
One of the most popular through trains was the Skipton-Manchester Victoria service, which called at principal stations like Colne, Nelson, Burnley, Rose Grove, Accrington and Bury. In May 1955 a north-bound train is seen on this service with three-cylinder 'Compound' 4-4-0 No 41061, another of the Manningham engines that worked regular turns down into Lancashire. *Gordon Coultas*

Left:
A considerably older view at Colne station illustrates a Midland Pullman car and Diagram D397 horse-box. These are being attached or detached from what appears to be a regular service train, and the tail lamp has been put on to the platform before being placed on the back of the rear coach. From this one might assume that this is a private party, possibly about to convey the elegant looking group at the end of the platform. *Colne Library*

Skipton or had through carriages. This was apparently welcomed by generations of workers and students who travelled daily into Keighley, and continued to do so down to the end of the service — all except for those who had boarded at Elslack which was to close completely in 1952.

Besides its value as a commuter route into the major towns, the Colne branch enjoyed more celebrated trains, indeed, prior to the completion of the Blackburn-Hellifield line, the Midland's crack 'Manchester-Scotch' expresses were routed this way. This was not all, for express traffic over the route was sustained and continued down to the very end, particularly holiday traffic and excursions which found this a useful cross-country route. In my youthful days, I could get to Colne for half-a-crown return, and so it proved to be a popular destination, either for angling in the canal or 'spotting' on the station. Usually I went equipped to do both, train-spotting being the secondary activity if the fish weren't biting or the weather turned inclement. On one of these occasions, a Saturday in July 1965, I 'copped' no less than 14 named engines passing on specials through Colne inside three hours, most making their way from the northeast to Blackpool or Southport. I had always intended to take a trip on the branch service to Barnoldswick on one of my jaunts, having had to miss out this section on a late-running railtour in May 1963. Unfortunately, there never seemed enough money to do both and when I was finally able to afford the extra 1s 5d fare in May 1966, I found that the branch passenger service had been withdrawn on 27 September previous — yet the so-and-so clerk at Huddersfield had still sold me a ticket. Infuriated at the loss of 3s 11d I complained most bitterly when I got back home, only to be told that 'stations were being closed with such frequent regularity, it was hard to keep track of things and that until the stocks of tickets were recalled they would still be issued'. As compensation I got a return ticket back to Earby the following month, and one for my bicycle, so in the end I did get to Barnoldswick. When I finally got there, I was rewarded with the sight of a Skipton-based 2-6-2T shunting three empty vans before vanishing back down the line moments later — Mecca proved to be an anti-climax!

The line from Skipton seemed safe, it was still well supported even though it was timetabled as two basic branch lines. Those who didn't know the area might have been deterred, the locals knew better. Beeching for once left the line alone, presumably recognising its importance to the local community as well as its strategic value as a diversionary route. Earby lost its goods traffic in March 1965, whilst the Barnoldswick pick-up goods trundled through from Skipton until the following August. Despite these withdrawals, the Government's 1967 White Paper on rail transport seemed to allow the passenger services' continued existence. However, in a shock announcement at the end of 1968 the line's demise was announced. Apparently no subsidy had been agreed to guarantee the line, support from the authorities for a railway cutting across the Lancashire-Yorkshire county boundary was, it seemed, the other chap's responsibility. Closure was rushed through with an astonishing, and almost disgusting, speed, so that the last train ran on 31 January 1970 severing the last rail link between West Yorkshire and East Lancashire. Today the trackbed to Colne stretches around 12 tantalising miles from Skipton; would it not make economic, environmental and above all commonsense to do something about it?

17 The East Lancashire Colne Branch

Conception and Construction

The southern approach to Colne owes its existence to a development primarily intended to link the town of Bury to Manchester, which in turn gave birth to the East Lancashire Railway. The Manchester, Bury & Rossendale Railway was formed in October 1843. The company's ultimate goal was to be the construction of a line from Clifton Junction (near Swinton) to Rawtenstall in the Rossendale Valley. An assured level of traffic was promised from the outset, with a large number of rapidly expanding textile manufacturing towns requiring a means of receiving supplies of raw cotton and wool. The company was authorised in 1844, and, whilst its proposed route north of Bury was intended as a single-track line, events were quickly to overtake the original plans. When the company promoted the Blackburn, Burnley, Accrington & Colne Extension Railway it was decided to build a double line of rails through to Stubbins Junction where the two routes would diverge. The two companies were amalgamated to form the East Lancashire Railway in November 1844, the name receiving Parliamentary sanction the following July.

Whilst the ELR achieved its initial goal by constructing a line down the Irwell Valley to Manchester, the free flow of traffic into Manchester was always going to be a problem. Events in the legendary battle of Clifton Junction prove this to be true, so there is little wonder that the company wanted an independent route to Liverpool (the main port into which supplies of raw cotton were then being shipped). That was to be provided with a line west through Blackburn and Preston. However, there was another route which the company wanted develop. This was an outlet to the east coast ports, for much of the cotton industry's export production went to central and eastern Europe. So it is this leg, the northward projection of the ELR from Accrington to Colne, that is of immediate concern to us. It first ran east to Rose Grove and thus into Burnley, where the line would turn almost due north before heading for Nelson and Colne. The most important structure on the line was the 21-arch Accrington Viaduct which, from the outset, was to prove a major headache due to subsidence problems. As work progressed on the viaduct it became evident that problems were beginning to appear and, despite underpinning, the structure was too heavy

Left:
Just south of Burnley Barracks station was the point on the East Lancashire Railway's branch line to Colne which was to become Gannow Junction, when the L&YR line from Todmorden to Burnley connected with the line from Accrington opened in 1850. Once a major junction, its role has been considerably simplified in recent years. Having just left Rose Grove, a two-car DMU threads its way over the junction and gains the Burnley-Colne line on 1 March 1986. *Paul D. Shannon*

for the ground on which it stood and it had to be demolished. This caused some delay whilst it was rebuilt, frustrating the hopes of a connection with the Midland at Colne. Even then the problems were not over, because by 1866 it had become unsafe again and required replacement, the new viaduct being ready by September 1867.

The ELR opened as far as Burnley Barracks in September 1848, with things on song for an end of the year join-up at Colne; but problems with another viaduct were to raise their ugly head. This time it was the viaduct on the approach to Burnley Bank Top station, which delayed the opening of the next section until December. Despite all these set-backs, the ELR reached Burnley nearly a year ahead of the rival L&YR branch from Todmorden — some small victory after the debacle at Clifton Junction. Even so, it was considered prudent to

construct a connecting branch between the two rail-ways, and this opened in September 1850. The ELR, meanwhile, forged on to Colne, but once again not without trouble. Difficulties with their contractor compounded the problems, the after affects causing rumblings that were to last several years, but eventually the ELR made an end-on junction with the Midland branch on 1 February 1849. Services to Skipton began at once and before long trains were running through on the ELR route to Liverpool, finally providing a competing railway service on a route which more or less paralleled the Leeds-Liverpool Canal.

The Line Described

From Accrington the stations were Huncoat, Hapton, and Rose Grove (for Padiham), followed by the two Burnley stations, but we begin our journey

description at Burnley Bank Top. The station lay to the east of 15-arch stone viaduct, which was the bottom of a continuous descent from Rose Grove. From here the tracks began to climb, 1 in 144 at first, which then eased slightly to 1 in 150. Presently the line arrived Marsden (later Brierfield), where a brick-built viaduct of five 40ft spans was situated. A mile and a quarter further on came Nelson, a grim blot on the landscape which had the redeeming feature of Pendle Hill (witches and all?) to provide an attractive backdrop. Heading north-east from Nelson the line pressed on towards Colne, passing over the shallow valley of Colne Water via a stone viaduct of six spans. The station was a typical Midland structure, functional but never grand, the main objective was always through traffic and freight — a large warehouse adjacent to the station bearing mute witness to the truth of this statement. Scenically, the line is much the same

today, except that it was completely singled between Burnley and Chaffers Siding signalbox at the end of 1986; the section beyond there being singled at an earlier date.

Services and Demise

From its inception the ELR was to prove itself to be a valuable cross-country route, linking North and East Lancashire to the industrial West Riding and beyond. The traffic patterns and trading routes established by the Leeds-Liverpool Canal provided a considerable boost to the embryonic railway, with consignments being switched from barge to railway wagon, but still following the same basic route. The ELR might have been a thorn in the L&YR's flesh, but they proved themselves to be a valuable freight artery for the mill towns in the north. In 1851 the first mention of an amalgamation between the ELR and L&YR were muted, but this was not achieved

Right:
A typical mixture of East Lancashire Railway architecture and L&YR embellishment is pictured in this view at Brierfield station. There is little by way of a clue to dating this picture, but the rake of wagons up by the goods shed are mostly high-sided private owner vehicles. *B. C. Lane Collection*

Below right:
Representative of the local services between Burnley and Colne in the 1950s, this view captures Aspinall 2-4-2T No 50653 leading a two-coach push-pull set. The coaches are of LNWR origin and had come to the branch from North Wales as replacement for the Newton Heath-built railmotor coaches which had been converted to work with the 2-4-2Ts during the 1930s after the withdrawal of the Hughes railmotor locomotives. *J. Porter*

Bottom right:
Westbound with a Manchester express, 2-6-4T No 42110 hurries along with its five-coach train. This service was extremely well patronised by local people, who commuted daily into the city or travelled there regularly in connection with their business. This included many people in the cotton-spinning and garment making trades; those who would make the same trip today would have to travel via Blackburn. *J. Porter*

until 13 August 1859. Understandably, it was the ELR's main allies, the Midland who had the most to loose, but the LNWR were also involved in the opposition that was to delay Parliamentary Authorisation for the amalgamation.

After amalgamation had finally gone through there was little change in the motive power scene, with ELR 2-4-0 and 0-6-0 tender engines operating the bulk of the services. Passenger trains over the ELR were basically aimed at providing an east-west route from Yorkshire to Preston via Todmorden, with a north-south artery from Manchester to Colne and into the Aire Valley. Central to this concept was a major junction offering suitable connection facilities at Rose Grove and to a lesser extent at Accrington. Peak hour services on the Colne branch were extremely well patronised, as were the through trains and the long distance services originating in North Lancashire. Unfortunately, the intermediate services were quite the reverse, with a competing tram service between Burnley and Colne taking many of the passengers. The trains got smaller and smaller in size, with most midday trains being operated by a 2-4-2T and a single coach. Occasionally two-coach trains were operated, but there was never really the clientèle to support them. Operating costs became paramount and so the L&YR decided to introduce a more economical form of working, and opted for an experimental railmotor which had recently been introduced on the Taff Vale Railway in Wales. The design was attributed to that line's Chief Mechanical Engineer, T. Hurry Riches, but the diminutive locomotives were built by Kerr Stuart of Stoke.

The L&YR ordered two of the railmotor locos and these were delivered in 1905. When built, they had 9in x 14in cylinders, but these were later adapted to 10½in x 14in by Horwich Works. The wheels were 3ft 6in in diameter. The trailer coach was 45ft by 9ft wide, offering a motorman's position, guard's compartment and seating for 48 passengers. The L&YR tried the first one between Bury and Tottington in July 1905 and it may have been used on the Colne service for a brief spell shortly thereafter. Accordingly, the L&YR implemented a railmotor construction programme on the basis of the economies such services offered and, from September 1906, the off-peak Burnley-Colne service was so worked. By converting to railmotor operation the company were able to provide new rail-level halts at Bott Lane, Reedley Hallows and New Hall Bridge, passengers boarding and alighting by means of retractable steps on the motor trailers. At an early stage in the proceedings the railmotor service was extended beyond Burnley to Rose Grove, thereby linking into the apex of the railway crossroads.

The railmotors continued on the service up to the early 1930s, but the locomotives needed a higher level of maintenance than conventional engines and, as the trailer units were maintained by Newton Heath Carriage Works and the locomotives attended to at Horwich, this immediately caused problems. It was therefore not uncommon to see the articulated end of a railmotor trailer coach propped up on baulks of timber at the end of one of the shed roads at Rose Grove, indicating that its engine was away at Horwich for repairs. The problems contin-

Below:
Heading for Burnley, Class 2P 'Compound' 4-4-0 trundles along recently-ballasted track with a four-coach stopping train. The train has just left Colne and will form the 4.42pm to Blackburn. *J. Porter*

Above:
What an awful contrast to the neat pictures we have seen before as Colne station reaches its lowest ebb. Taken in August 1976, the picture shows the terminus of the line from Burnley, just a single platform, a vandalised bus-shelter and a set of notice-boards that are conspicuous by the absence of notices. Since this picture was taken there have been a few minor improvements, but not many. *Gordon Coultas*

ued to grow as the units aged, and eventually the railmotors were withdrawn and the LMS introduced 2-4-2Ts fitted for pull-push operation. Frugal as ever the LMS did not produce new stock, but merely converted the old railmotor trailers for a new use. In many ways this was a logical move as the trailers were already fitted with vacuum controls for driver operation, so despite their antiquity they lasted down into the era of the DMUs that were eventually to supplant them.

One aspect of the Colne branch was the service to London (Euston), which had diminished to a through coach service by the end of the 1950s, but was nevertheless still very well supported. For example, John Dawson a former textile company traveller recalls that 'it was always a busy train on a Monday, there usually being two first-class coaches and two seconds, the train was always full of mill owners, directors and travellers going up to town on business, booking was nearly always essential, and it was the same coming back on a Friday'. For some inexplicable reason BR failed to reinstate this service after it was 'temporarily withdrawn' to allow the Manchester-Crewe electrification to take place. Not only this, but there then came a further cut-back in the DMU workings which got worse and worse as time went on. Even though the trains into Manchester were still reasonably well used, the service died with the Beeching-orientated closure of the line between Accrington and Bury in December 1966. After this the businessmen wanting to go

to London were forced to go to Preston, Leeds or Bradford instead of Manchester. After this things just got worse and worse as passenger trains were cut back and goods facilities withdrawn, before eventually culminating in the closure of the line through to Skipton which we outlined in the previous chapter. Today a light-weight DMU plods along the line from Colne, usually travelling through to Preston or Blackpool South. The railway it travels upon has been savagely pruned until there is so little left that it is not worth talking about, the miles of sidings that it once spawned now have been torn away. The freight traffic that gave it life is nowhere to be seen, unless you happen to proceed beyond Burnley Bank Top, now optimistically named Central, to Rose Grove. If you get off the train here you cannot fail to see where the freight traffic has gone; it is still there, speeding past you along the M65 motorway which runs adjacent to the railway.

18 The Grassington Branch

Conception and Construction

It is, perhaps, appropriate to conclude our narrative with a look at a railway which holds a unique distinction, in that it was British Railway's last steam-worked branch line. It might even be said, like the Glossop branch, that this is not a South Pennine line at all, as it penetrates well inside the Yorkshire Dales National Park. Whilst that is true, it is representative of branch lines on the upper-fringe of the South Pennines, as well as being a remarkably interesting survivor. Some may ask why I have chosen this line to represent the Dales branches, the straight facts are that this is a little bit of personal prejudice and favouritism — and after all, with the publisher's permission, it is my book.

The history of the Grassington branch has to be set in context with other developments in the area, not least the construction of the railway from Leeds and Bradford to Skipton which was discussed in Chapter 16. This line took the Midland to the capital of the dales and, with further acquisitions and developments, it became part of a main line to North Lancashire, Cumbria and Scotland. A lesser known development was the 11½ miles of railway from Ilkley to Skipton, which were authorised by an Act of Parliament on 16 July 1883. The line opened five years later, and soon became a popular route for tourists, most of whom made for the delights of Bolton Abbey. Even the North Eastern Railway got in on the act, by running a regular series of tourist trains from York. Yet, underlying all these developments, was a much stronger desire — the construction of a through main line from Lancashire to the northeast of England. This was particularly important as, at that time, the carriage of goods between these two important industrial centres involved sending traffic through one of two major bottle-necks — York or Carlisle.

The first attempt to take a line this way came in the form of the Liverpool, Manchester & Newcastle-upon-Tyne Junction Railway in 1846. With the tacit backing of the M&L, this line would have diverged from the L&B at Elslack and run, via Grassington, up to Kettlewell and Buckden. At Crook Gill it would have dived into a tunnel nearly three miles long to reach Bishopdale near Kidstone. A short branch would have been projected to a lead smelter in the dale, and an intermediate station pro-

Left:
The continued use of Grassington & Threshfield station as a destination for tourist trains had been its saving grace, preventing the complete abandonment that was evident at stations like Kirkburton which had closed to passengers around the same time. Even today there could be an environmental case to argue for the retention of lines such as this for special traffic — at least it would relieve the massive pressure on local roads in the summer months. On 16 June 1968 No D5113 is being called forward so it can run-round its train, having worked an RCTS special along the branch. *Gavin Morrison*

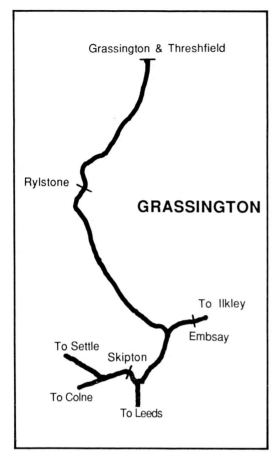

Grassington & Threshfield

Rylstone

GRASSINGTON

To Ilkley

Embsay

To Settle
Skipton

To Colne

To Leeds

such a scheme to come to fruition at this late stage in the railway development era, but it was decided that the first stage of the route could be built as far as Grassington. Authority was gained in the private-sponsored Yorkshire Dales Railway Act of August 1897, and the eight miles of railway from Embsay opened on 29 July 1902.

The Line Described
Leaving what was Platform No 5 at Skipton station, the route for Grassington took the Ilkley line which began to climb up a fairly steep artificial embankment as soon as it left the station. This was needed to achieve an overbridge above the line to Leeds and Bradford, as well as a crossing of the Leeds-Liverpool Canal. In winter months, when the rails were wet or greasy, spectacular results could be witnessed on this short and sharp gradient. Unfortunately, the sort of cameras and film we could afford in those days were not up to capturing these unforgettable events. Running northeast along the fringe of Skipton's boundary the line presently rumbled through the 219yd long Haw Bank Tunnel to come to Embsay Junction, beyond where the scenic route to Ilkley turned to the east. A bit of that line, which closed in 1965, is still there and operated by steam trains. The Yorkshire Dales Railway Society reopened a 1½ mile section of the line on 19 May 1979 and is progressively extending its line towards the closed station at Bolton Abbey. The Yorkshire Dales Railway has since become known as the 'friendly railway' due to the courtesy and consideration it shows to its visitors. Though just a two-mile long line today, one suspects that the YDR look covetously upon the Grassington branch with a view to its acquisition if BR should ever decide to pull out.

Leaving the junction, the branch heads northwest, passing through a substantial cutting near Ellergill. For the next mile it runs parallel with Eller Beck, until it encounters a level crossing with the road leading to Crookrise Wood. Immediately beyond this, the line crosses over the Beck and begins to run along its western side. A deep cutting is then encountered, with an over-line road bridge carrying the B6265. Road, river and railway then run parallel with each other for over a mile, until the branch negotiates a large crescent-shaped curve to reach the village of Rylstone, where the line's only intermediate station was once located. From Rylstone the line runs north, but where it crosses a minor road on the level it then turns northeast for the last three miles to Grassington (10 miles from Skipton). After passing the village of Cracoe, the line comes alongside the B6265 once again to reach the Swinden Limestone Works, where the line has terminated since 1969. Today a green sward is all that is left to continue up to Grassington, but the

vided at Thoralby & Newbiggin. Continuing down the side of Bishopdale Beck the line would eventually reach and cross the River Ure before finally connecting with the Wensleydale line near Redmire. However, the intervention of the infamous George Hudson prevented the line becoming reality and, thus, the railway world was denied a line that would have rivalled the Settle & Carlisle for its rugged scenic grandeur.

However, like all good ideas, it did not die an instant death, for the spark kept burning and smouldering in the minds of both locals and railway promoters alike. Accordingly it reappeared in the the 1860s, 1880s and 1890s. In the latter set of proposals, a line was envisaged running from Hellifield to Grassington and up Wharfedale. At Kettlewell it was to deviate from the earlier plans and fork into the small valley, running northeast to Starbotton. A much longer tunnel would then have been carved below Starbotton Fell, emerging somewhere near Bradley in Coverdale. Pressing down Coverdale it would cross the Wensleydale line near Leyburn, then continue through to join the ECML just south of Darlington. In reality it was too much to expect

Left:
The line's passenger service vanished in the days of the LMS, and surrounding services went in the 1960s, but the Grassington line went on to be Britain's last steam worked branch line. Even in this day and age, where freight traffic is being forcibly ejected on to the roads by high pricing policies, the Grassington branch is still well-used for the carriage of limestone from Swinden Quarries — elements of which are shown in this March 1967 view. *Gavin Morrison*

Below left:
With the quarry buildings just in view through the arch of bridge No 32, the Grassington branch is pictured in 1950. At this time the rails still reached all the way to the terminus. *David Ibbotson*

Left:
The Yorkshire Dales Railway between Ilkley and Skipton was another of the secondary railway routes which did not figure in the Macmillan Government's plans for a revised national railway network. Discarded by Beeching, part of it still survives as a preserved line today, but how much more could have been attained had the scenic rail route been left in position. At the junction with the Grassington branch at Embsay, the YDR has just been reached by No D5113 which has completed its tour of the branch on 16 June 1968. *Gavin Morrison*

Above:
One of the real delights of the line down to Grassington was bridge No 37 — Ings Bridge, Linton. From the left-hand side of the picture, pedestrians would climb a gentle slope up to the crown of the bridge; beyond this a flight of steps led down to the footpath through the fields. Lacking in railway action this view might be, but it should have loads of appeal for the railway modelling fraternity. *David Ibbotson*

Below:
On 6 October 1965, Skipton shed's Standard Class 4 4-6-0 No 75042 sits in the platform at Grassington & Threshfield. The passenger service might have ended 35 years earlier, but you could be forgiven for not believing this fact due to the tidy state of the station. Sadly, despite the smiling face on the 4-6-0's smoke-box door, this engine was not one of the class which survived into preservation. *Gavin Morrison*

trackbed is easily traced. Yet, this still holds some pleasant surprises, as for example, some of the line's attractive footbridges survive.

On reaching Grassington the line reached an attractive little terminus, but it was some distance from the centre of the village. An inn near the station no doubt did good business after the arrival of the branch train, supplying the necessary fortification for the walk up to the village. However, in view of the intended extension up the dale, this was the only place that the 'temporary' terminus could have been built. Whilst this was acceptable as long as there was a chance of an extension, its inconvenient location was one of the contributory factors in the poor support that ultimately led to the withdrawal of passenger services. Had the railway decided that Grassington was a sufficient enough objective in its own right, it would have made a more suitable terminus that would have probably endeared itself to the visitors who flocked into the dales.

Services and Demise
The first passenger trains ran to Grassington & Threshfield on 29 July 1902, when Midland 0-4-4T No 1536 was specially decked out for the celebrations. The service was basic but effective, with the Midland 0-4-4Ts working the line from the outset. However, the line maintained its nominal independence until the 1923 Grouping. There were seven trains a day, with an extra one on Saturdays. There was even a Sunday service of two trains. The first down train left Skipton at 6.55am and the last up train left Grassington at 7.14am. All the workings were out and back from Skipton and, as a result, few empty stock workings were seen. The average journey took 26min in the up direction and between 27 and 29min down, though the first train of the day from Grassington took a whole 32min due to the extra time allowed for loading milk churns at Rylstone. From 1910 onwards, a slip coach for Grassington was attached/detached from the residential express service which ran between Morecambe and Bradford in a morning and back again every evening. This was aimed particularly at the mill-owners and wool merchants who escaped the smoky confines of the city at the end of a day's industrious activity and enjoyed residence in the fresh ozone of sea breezes or the bracing air of the Yorkshire Dales. This service continued right down to the demise of the branch passenger service, which came as the Depression of the 1930s affected the viability of many rural lines.

With the end of the summer season, the branch was closed to scheduled passenger services on 27 September 1930, much to the annoyance of local residents and the Bradford businessmen who had settled in Upper Wharfedale. With the line's demise three 0-4-4Ts stationed at Skipton shed were transferred elsewhere, whilst the antiquated set of clerestory stock was put into store. The local press captured the resentment, with one letter stating 'Betrayed by the LMS — The discontinuation of the passenger railway to Grassington is symptomatic of the attitude of today manifested by the big railway companies, big they may be, but not in their magnanimity. Profit is all their morals impinge upon, and if a line of railway does not show a profit, it is of no use to them. We see all too clearly that the Yorkshire Dales Railways is such a line upon which great profits must be made, or it is one which must put forth its head into the hangman's noose. But what the great LMS may not appreciate in its decimation of the little Grassington line, is that many influential people live in the district serviced by this 'inconsequential backwater'. It is we who have supported the great railway companies over many years past, it is we who have been its shareholders, it is we who have provided the finance to make them what they are. The London Midland and Scottish company will learn this to their great regret, for shabby treatment begets its own just deserts.' Strong words indeed, but ones which eloquently portray the argument of a social need for railways, and perhaps nowhere was a social railway more needed than in a valley like Upper Wharfedale.

However, the death of the passenger service did not mean the end of passenger trains, quite the contrary. From 1930 onwards a steady stream of excursion trains made their way up the dale, including a number of LNER trains from Harrogate and York. Ramblers' trains also became quite popular, whilst during the war a number of troop trains were seen along the branch when the army used the nearby hills as training grounds. Yet it was the agricultural

Above:
Taken from a different angle, the Standard Class 4 is seen from the far side of the run-round loop as it sits in the platform. Yet, despite its quaint appeal, this picture shows how impractical goods transport had become by this time. The locomotive with its 25,100lb of tractive effort, a two-man crew and a guard is surely uneconomic for the two wagons and two guard's vans that comprise the return load. This was the sort of scene that dismayed Richard Beeching; a cure *was* needed, but the drastic surgery that was applied was surely an over-reaction. *Gavin Morrison*

freight, sustained by mineral traffic, that kept the line alive. By the end of the war the freight services had diminished slightly, but it was still sufficient to have a daily pick-up goods working as well as specials to the quarries. The Ilkley-Skipton line went over to DMU operation at the end of the 1950s but,

Right:
Setting the Grassington branch in its true scene amongst the rolling foothills of the Pennines and the Yorkshire Dales: on 5 August 1986 Class 31s, Nos 31205 and 31185, pass down the branch with the 6E63 10.39 Rylstone-Hull Dairycoates working which contains 11 Tilcon hopper wagons. Note the large 'S' curve in the track formation to the rear of the train.
Paul D. Shannon

The end of the line, both for this book and the present Grassington branch, as HST power car No 43064 comes to a rest close to the branch line buffer stops on 26 January 1991. Tourists may no longer be able to reach Grassington by rail, but the demand is surely there. If railway enthusiasts are willing to pay good money to travel to an industrial setting like Swinden Quarry, how much more so would the average traveller be prepared to make a pleasant journey on through the countryside to Grassington. *Gavin Morrison*

despite this minor revolution, that line became another Beeching Era casualty. The passenger service was withdrawn on 22 March 1965, with goods traffic ceasing between Ilkley and Embsay on 5 July that year. Ironically, the goods service down the branch to Grassington remained extant, and was not to be withdrawn until 11 August 1969 — a whole year after the demise of BR steam workings.

Skipton MPD, which had so long provided the locomotives for working the branch, closed on 3 April 1967. Thereafter responsibility for the operation of the services came to rest on the shoulders of distant Carnforth shed. The engines which had been working from Skipton, Riddles 2-6-0s Nos 75026/41/2/58/9, went over to Lancashire. These continued to work the Grassington branch for a short while but, by 1968, the duties had fallen to a regular trio of Standard Class 4s, Nos. 75019/27/48 — of which No.75027 went on to be preserved. Working the dwindling pick-up goods or the trains of ballast wagons to Swinden

Quarry, the 2-6-0s enjoyed the twilight of British steam. I had first come to the line on board a Yorkshire Dales Rail Tour behind ex-LNER Class K4 *The Great Marquess* in May 1963, but the train's late arrival back in Bradford meant that I had to get out at Skipton and never got to complete the tour which included a trip to the 'fabled' Barnoldswick. However, having been captivated by the brief visit to Grassington, walking and cycling in the dales saw my frequent return to the youth hostel at Kettlewell. By the age of 16, and with a few bob in my pocket and bike or rucksack dumped in the luggage van, the train was regularly taken to Skipton. Some weekends were strenuous affairs, heading high into the dales, usually around the route of the S&C; some weekends were spent rock climbing — but more than a few were spent watching the last days of steam on the Grassington branch.

The line is still extant as far as the Tilcon works at Swinden Quarry and, with the recent decision to give the company a substantial Section 8 grant to improve facilities, the stone traffic should last well into the next century.

However, to the author, the line has lost many of its attractions. The modern freight locomotives that work on this pretty branch present little appeal, and even the occasional rail tours (which have seen Inter City 125s along the branch) hold little magic for me personally. Perhaps it is just an idiosyncratic feeling, but I for one prefer to remember the Grassington branch as I did the other Pennine branches —a line of rural charm, and steam engines. The fact this was the country's last steam worked branch line (outside preservation) makes it just that bit more special.